Listening In

Listening In

Cybersecurity in an Insecure Age

SUSAN LANDAU

Yale UNIVERSITY PRESS

New Haven and London

Yale University Press books may be purchased in quantity for educational, business, or promotional use. For information, please e-mail sales.press@yale.edu (U.S. office) or sales@yaleup.co.uk (U.K. office).

Set in Minion type by Integrated Publishing Solutions, Grand Rapids, Michigan.
Printed in the United States of America.

Library of Congress Control Number: 2017944412
ISBN 978-0-300-22744-4 (hardcover : alk. paper)

A catalogue record for this book is available from the British Library.

This paper meets the requirements of ANSI/NISO Z39.48-1992 (Permanence of Paper).

10 9 8 7 6 5 4 3 2 1

*Dedicated to my walking buddies—both two- and four-legged—
without whom this book would not have been written.*

Contents

Preface

In February 2016 the Judiciary Committee of the US House of Representatives invited me to testify on encryption. Cryptography protects data in motion—communications—and data at rest—particularly data stored on smartphones, laptops, and other digital devices—from prying eyes. The encryption issue has bedeviled US law enforcement since the early 1990s. Because encryption was becoming a default on consumer devices, law enforcement's worst fears were finally coming true. Not only were smart criminals and terrorists using encryption to hide their plans, as they had been doing so for quite some time, but now the less savvy ones were as well.[1]

FBI director James Comey was pressing Congress to require that "exceptional access" be built into encryption systems, enabling law enforcement to access communications or open devices with legal authorization. But the FBI's seemingly simple request was anything but. If you make it easier to break into a communication system or a phone, it's not just government agents with a court order who will get in. Bad guys, including criminals and other sophisticated attackers, will also take advantage of the system. Weakening security is exactly the wrong move for a world fully dependent on digital communications and devices to conduct personal, business, and government affairs.

This argument is not new; for quite some time my colleagues and I have been saying that security—personal, business, and national security—requires widespread use of strong encryption systems. That means encryption systems without back doors, front doors, or any other form of easy access. But while encryption undoubtedly makes investigations harder to conduct, law enforcement has alternative tools at its disposal. This was the message I was bringing to Congress.

The congressional hearing played out against the background of a dispute between Apple and the FBI involving a locked iPhone. In December 2015, two terrorists in San Bernardino, California, killed fourteen members of the county Health Department. The terrorists themselves were killed in a shootout, but the FBI recovered extensive evidence related to their plans, including an Apple iPhone issued by the county to one of the perpetrators, who had been employed by the Health Department. The FBI sought to have Apple write software to unlock the phone's security protections. When the company refused to do so, the law enforcement agency took Apple to court, which initially ruled in the government's favor.

At the Judiciary Committee hearing, James Comey railed against "warrant-proof" spaces and the difficulties locked devices presented to keeping Americans safe. Apple's general counsel and I presented a different narrative: in a world of increasing cyberattacks, communications and data required stronger protections. Weakening them is the last thing we should be doing. Surely the FBI could find other ways to open the phone —essentially hacking in under a court order (a practice known as "lawful hacking")—without making Apple undo its security protections, thus putting other phones at risk.[2]

Discussion raged for weeks. Which approach offers more security? Forcing Apple to undo the protections the company had carefully designed for the iPhone? Or leaving these protections in place, potentially not accessing the terrorists' communications, but leaving everyone else's phone secure? Then, after having testified in court and in Congress that only Apple could undo the phone's security protections, the FBI had a surprise announcement. Law enforcement didn't need Apple's help after all; a contractor had found a way to unlock the phone. The immediate problem of Apple's secure phone went away.

The problem of that particular iPhone had been resolved, but the FBI's fear of "going dark"—of losing the ability to listen in or collect data when this information was encrypted—remained. As spring turned to summer, I found myself explaining over and over the complexities of our digital world—how much we stored on our devices, how much data was at risk, how easy it was to break into systems, and how useful phones might be for authenticating ourselves and thus preventing that theft. Our cybersecurity risks have intensified over the last two decades as the Internet has become an integral part of people's personal and business lives. In the wake of the Judiciary Committee hearing, I spoke on this topic in Washington, DC, California, South Korea, and Germany; at the National September 11 Memorial and Museum; and on NPR and the BBC. But it was clear that many more people needed to understand the complexities and risks of the situation than I could reach with my talks. I decided to write this book.

That was August 2016. But even as I was writing, the story was changing in remarkable ways. For decades policymakers believed the main cyberthreats were the theft of data from business and the government and possible attacks on computer systems controlling critical infrastructure. In September 2015 a low-level FBI operative called the Democratic National Committee (DNC) to alert them that their network had been hacked. His message was given low priority. Although he called again and again, the FBI agent was essentially ignored. By the time the DNC and US intelligence agencies woke up to the seriousness of the problem, it was too late.[3]

The Russians, who have long used disinformation as a technique for influencing events, turned the tools of cyberexploitation against the Democratic Party and, in particular, Hillary Clinton's presidential candidacy. Using common forms of cyberattack, the Russians stole emails from the DNC, the Democratic Congressional Campaign Committee, and from the private account of John Podesta (chair of Clinton's presidential campaign). The email leak, combined with false news stories that were favorable to Republican candidate Donald Trump and unfavorable to Clinton—and Twitter bots that brought them much attention—were new forms of disruption. The leaks and false news drove US press stories and attention, creating a very negative effect for Clinton in the waning days of the 2016 election. This Russian attack was different from anything the United States had anticipated when the military had practiced cyberwar games.[4]

The issue of cybersecurity was no longer only about preventing Chinese hackers from stealing fighter plane plans to use for their own military, or about the US military's use of sophisticated cyberattack weapons to destroy centrifuges at an Iranian nuclear facility (as discussed in the chapters that follow). Now it was about protecting vastly larger swathes of society—the press, universities, research organizations (the latter two had been targeted by Russia during the campaign). Now cybersecurity was about extending strong forms of security to everyone.[5]

When the FBI supports exceptional access, and tech companies resist it, the FBI is not weighing the demands of security versus privacy. Rather, it is pitting questions about the efficiency and effectiveness of law enforcement against our personal, business, and national security. Instead of security versus privacy, this is an argument of security versus security. And although the FBI's goals are to improve law enforcement's ability to conduct investigations, the proposed means—weakening encryption and the security of phones—risk a far greater harm.

The encryption debate, a subject that previously occupied only techies and policy wonks, has now become critically important to national security. How do we secure ourselves in the face of the Digital Revolution, in which our world is increasingly being controlled through bits? This revolution has brought humanity tremendous economic, technological, scientific, and cultural benefits. But it also provides bad actors with the ability to steal and disrupt at a distance, performing serious mischief at scale.

We've lived with these risks since the 1980s, but the cyberthreats are now far more serious—and cybersecurity protections, including encrypted communications and secured communications, are far more critical now than they were even a half-decade ago. We have the option to press companies to develop secure and private systems, or to provide systems that make it easier for law enforcement and national security to conduct investigations. However, the latter increases the risk that others will take advantages of the weaknesses present in such "exceptional access." We need to make the right decision, for our safety, long-term security, and humanity.

To help readers understand what's at stake, I begin this account with two chapters that explore how and why the Digital Revolution has progressed faster than society's ability to keep up with the changes. These changes have produced new kinds of threats, which I explore in detail in Chapter 3. In Chapter 4, I discuss different ways by which we can secure both our data and the networked systems that depend on it. But that very security complicates investigators' jobs—that's the whole fight right there—so in Chapter 5, I look at how law enforcement investigations can work even when encrypted communications and locked devices are ubiquitous. The concluding chapter takes a hard look at the challenges cyberthreats present to open, dynamic societies—and the decisions we must make to preserve them.

Listening In

1

Racing into the Digital Revolution

We used to live in a world in which a farmer grabbed a handful of soil to determine whether it was damp, a pedestrian hailed a taxi through a wave of her arm, a tourist traveled by plane to see a foreign city's streets, and an auto manufacturer mass-produced repair parts. Today, soil sensors report moisture levels via the Internet, apps like Uber allow strangers to "share" rides, Google Street View lets you explore streets of Seoul and Paris on your phone, and 3D printers produce plastic spare parts for Mercedes Benz.[1]

The Agricultural Revolution transformed human communities from hunter-gathers to an agrarian society. The Industrial Revolution urbanized us. We are now in the midst of a third revolution, the Digital Revolution. We have replaced the world of atoms with the world of bits.

Humans take time to absorb change. Our first instinct is to describe new technologies in terms of things we know: trains are iron horses; cars, horseless carriages. These analogies can be useful, such as when a steam train travels twice as fast as a horse. They are misleading if the train travels several hundred miles an hour.

The Digital Revolution is moving several thousand miles an hour, and the consequences are profound. But except for a handful of philosophers, futurists, engineers, and venture capitalists, it's usually only when something goes wrong—when a server fails and an airline cancels hundreds of flights, or when you are driving in a remote region and must rely on a paper map—that the rest of us may stop and realize how rapid this transformation has been. Yet over and over we find it irresistible to grab that shiny new toy—the Uber app that enables us to summon a ride that whisks us to our destination. Only later do we stop to reckon the social consequences—the costs of that action in terms of costs to labor and public transport. We're letting norms evolve without thinking about the consequences, for our safety or our humanity.

Computers have been tied to national security ever since their use in World War II, when their calculations enabled shipboard anti-aircraft weapons to target enemy aircraft. But it was in code breaking that computers first proved critical. The British Colossus machine at Bletchley Park cracked the German Lorenz cipher, providing invaluable insights into the enemy's thinking. This knowledge enabled the Allies to successfully deceive Germany about plans for the D-Day invasion, a deception that was crucial to the mission's success—and to Germany's defeat.[2]

During the 1950s computers lifted the burden of both heavy number crunching—taking months off the design of airplanes, improving the accuracy of weather prediction, modeling atomic weapons—and prosaic business tasks. Britain's Lyons

Tea company, for instance, used its computer to determine its production schedule, including the delivery of tea cakes to its shops. Most businesses, though, still relied on people, adding machines, and typewriters.

Computers shouldered more responsibility in the 1960s, when IBM developed its System 360. The IBM 360 performed the calculations that sent men to the moon—and brought them back. Those calculations enabled the lunar landing module to "rendezvous" with an orbiting rocket, essential if the astronauts aboard were to return to earth. Exciting as the moon shot was, the IBM 360's more mundane applications may have had a larger impact. Because the machine could handle large amounts of data, it was widely adopted by banks and other financial institutions. Prior to the advent of business computing, for instance, borrowers knew best whether they could pay back a loan. Now, using computers and information sharing across financial institutions, banks could carry out their own calculations to assess the risk of default for a potential borrower. Suddenly banks had the upper hand, using increased access to data to decide whom to back and whom to charge higher interest rates. The balance between customers and the banks shifted in favor of financial institutions; one result was the 1970 Fair Credit Reporting Act, which gave consumers access to and rights over their credit reports. This effort to redress the balance between people and lending institutions was the first of a stream of laws and regulations that would seek to protect people as computer technology changed their lives.

In the 1970s the price of computers began to drop and the machines moved onto the factory floor. Computer control was introduced into product planning, design, assembly, and delivery. Robots began to replace people for certain simple, highly mechanized tasks. In the 1980s, the arrival of word processing programs and spreadsheets began displacing typewriters and adding machines—and secretaries. By the 1990s, humans were still in charge on the factory floor, but fewer were needed. The opening of the Internet for commercial use that same decade brought yet more transformations for retail, journalism, and virtually every aspect of daily life.[3]

Over the decades, the Digital Revolution changed factories and offices. A more profound change to society began about ten years ago. With cellphones, we made ourselves accessible at any time, from any place. Facebook became publicly available in 2006; the iPhone, in 2007. The combination of social media and a device that you could carry with you proved irresistible. Ninety percent of South Koreans carry a smartphone, as do 77 percent of Australians, 72 percent of Americans, and 58 percent of Chinese. The populations of Spain, New Zealand, the United Kingdom, and Canada have embraced smartphones with similar enthusiasm. The revolution took place seemingly overnight. Today, almost all of us carry mobile computers, and we do so almost all the time.[4]

The Digital Revolution created vast social change. It has been responsible, for instance, for the massive shift of employment in the United States. Automation corresponded to a 250 percent gain in manufacturing productivity—and a simultaneous 46 percent decline in jobs—between 1980 and 2014. As a result, it takes half as many people to produce two-and-a-half times as many goods. Computer control and robots took these jobs away, not China.[5]

This revolution changed our daily lives in innumerable ways. The stolid black rotary-dial telephones that were in our parents' homes have been replaced by mobile devices that are with us twenty-four hours a day. The US president can reach out and tweet his message to followers, ignoring the press that previously dominated the transmission of news. Whole swathes of industries and businesses—including brick-and-mortar stores, manufacturers, even law firms—have been upended.

These transformations have tremendous implications for security and privacy, but most members of the public didn't grasp the extent of the changes until the Snowden revelations. In 2013, Edward Snowden's disclosure of the surveillance capabilities of the National Security Agency (NSA) revealed how much information was on computerized networks, and how valuable that information was to government authorities. In response to the public outcry over the surveillance, the US computer industry began taking the issue of securing users' information far more seriously. Communications are best secured with end-to-end encryption, cryptography that permits only the sender and recipient to see the unencrypted form of the message. Encryption can also secure the contents of a device, so if a smartphone or laptop is stolen, its encrypted files remain confidential. But the same techniques that provide security complicate law enforcement and national security investigations.

Encryption on its own will not solve the cybersecurity problem, but it is nonetheless a crucial technology for doing so. Indeed, the most technically sophisticated part of the US government—the intelligence agencies—agrees. A leaked 2009 cybersecurity document from the US National Intelligence Council warned that government and private-sector computers were vulnerable to attacks from other nations and criminals because encryption technologies were being deployed too slowly, while an accompanying table described encryption as the "[b]est defense to protect data" especially when combined with multifactor authentication, in which a user must input an additional credential after a password. The report concluded that the steps being taken by the US tech companies in increasing their use of encryption to protect communications and devices "would prevent the vast majority of intrusions."[6]

Thus, securing communications and devices puts different societal needs—needs that have changed dramatically since the onset of the Digital Revolution—on a collision course. On one side, government investigators need to be able to access some of the information contained in digital communications. On the other, the people need to be able to secure their communications and devices themselves. That conflict—and the need to find security in an age of cyberinsecurity—is the subject of this book. The information that we entrust to digital media and control is increasing at ever more rapid rates, as are the number and sophistication of the attacks. For this reason I believe our society is best served by securing communications and devices even if that choice makes government investigations more difficult—and I will show why in the following pages.

Humans are a highly social species. Internationally, 76 percent of Internet users access Facebook, Twitter, and other social applications. A smartphone makes it remarkably easy to respond instantly to calls, emails, and tweets. Social media apps make it hard not to succumb to doing so. Thus smartphones are always with us, and always on. While cellphones made it easy for people to be reached anytime and anyplace, smartphones made it easy to answer a work request from anywhere—the boarding line at an airport, a hotel check-in desk, or a restaurant.

A decade ago the line between work and home was relatively clear. Email or a call to a spouse or a friend might be answered during the workday on a work phone or computer, and a dedicated professional might receive a business call or email in the evening or on the weekend. But there were clear boundaries between the two, well worked out over time. Then the smartphone arrived.

At first, smartphones just offered phone calls, email, and music, but applications—apps—quickly started arriving. The BlackBerry, the first pocket-sized consumer phone to have email, was an early casualty of the smartphone juggernaut. In the mid-2000s, high-placed executives and government officials considered BlackBerrys essential. Members of the US defense establishment carried them, as did senior people in industry, including Google's CEO Eric Schmidt. German chancellor Angela Merkel's secure phone—the one that was not intercepted by the NSA—was a BlackBerry, as was Pakistani prime minister Nawar Sharif's. And in 2009, when newly elected President Barack Obama was unwilling to let go of his BlackBerry, the NSA reengineered it to make it more secure (losing lots of functionality along the way). But from its high point in the late 2000s to the mid-2010s, BlackBerry's share of the smartphone market dropped from 20 to under 1 percent.[7]

The problem was with what BlackBerrys couldn't do. You could make phone calls and send and receive email securely, and you could use certain Microsoft applications. But Black-Berrys didn't run apps: no Angry Birds, Snapchat, or this week's version of Pokémon Go. (The apps that were available were often locked out by the issuing company's information technology, or IT, department, which managed the devices.) Users who didn't need a secure phone opted for a smartphone that could load apps. And because these same users didn't want to carry two phones, they brought both their iPhones and Androids to work. They added their business email accounts and calendars to their personal phones, and forgot about their BlackBerrys.

Androids and iPhones became the repositories of crucial

day-to-day information, including emails, contact information; private intimate details, including photos, texts, and health data; and personal security information, for instance, bank accounts. The phones carried essential work information as well.

This was a social transformation that caught many people, both average users and security experts, by surprise. It created a serious new risk for companies, allowing proprietary data to escape the company's control. Now, employees accessed crucial, private data on unsecured personal phones that could easily go missing. This was just one more step on the trajectory that had begun when networks enabled people to easily move data from the workplace to home. But 1980s-style dialup modems at home were a far cry in speed and convenience from our current ability to connect. And that availability not only meant a new way of working anytime, anywhere, but a new way of removing data from corporations, governments, and even private individuals. Peril and ease were there in equal measure.

Security experts saw the risk and started offering solutions. Companies such as Cisco, for instance, began offering services that would put security software on smartphones, providing a managed space that kept corporate data secure even if the phone was taken. But such solutions only work if properly implemented, and often they are not.

Apple and the FBI would never have come to blows if the San Bernardino Health Department had implemented the mobile device management system it was paying for. The terrorists had smashed their personal phones, but the police found terrorist Syed Rizwan Farook's Health Department–issued iPhone. Six weeks before the shootings, Farook had manipulated the controls of this phone to shut off backups to Apple's iCloud. The department, meanwhile, had also been paying for a device management service, but it wasn't turned on. With neither of these systems in place, there was no automatic system working to ensure the information on the phone could be obtained. Investigators were particularly interested in obtaining information related to an unaccounted-for eighteen-minute gap between the time of the shootings and when police found the terrorists. The FBI wanted to know where Farook had been and whether he had communicated with anyone during that time.[8]

Apple's iOS 9 operating system enables encryption by default. Unless the phone is open and unlocked—and Farook's work iPhone was not—the data on the device is automatically encrypted. The key to unlock the phone data entangles the user's PIN (personal identification number) and the phone's hardware key, making knowledge of the PIN seemingly essential for anyone attempting to access data on the device. The FBI did not know the user PIN, and Apple's security protections were designed to thwart PIN guesses. Each time a user guesses an incorrect PIN on an iPhone running iOS 9, the phone delays the next try. After ten incorrect tries, the operating system erases the data on the phone. These features protect the phone if it is lost or stolen, but they also made it extremely difficult for the FBI to break into Farook's work iPhone.[9]

The FBI sought a court order requiring Apple to provide a software "update" for Farook's device. This update would undo the phone's security protections and would be personalized to this particular phone. The update would not itself break open the phone, but rather would allow the FBI to try all possible PINs, eventually unlocking the phone through "brute force" (see Chapter 4). A US district court initially ruled that Apple should assist the FBI. Arguing that the FBI's position was a legal overreach that would result in a back door to the iPhone that was "too dangerous to build," Apple fought the court order requiring the company to write this software (something that the company said would take six to ten highly specialized engineers two to four weeks to do). The company also appealed to the court of public opinion. There the FBI, which was seeking help to examine a terrorist's cellphone, ran into serious opposition. A significant portion of the US public thought Apple should not undo the phone's security protections. The court battled ended when a private contractor opened the phone for the FBI—but the fight over locked phones and encryption had entered a new, very public phase.[10]

In many ways the story of Syed Rizwan Farook's work iPhone is a rerun of the "First Crypto War" of the 1990s. The previous battle concerned what encryption could be exported in computer and communications equipment. Export controls came into place after World War II, a time when only military equipment used cryptography. By the late 1970s, cryptography was used in civilian applications, including by banks for wiring money; over time, even more types of industry were using cryptography. By the 1990s, industry leaders were pressuring government to lift the controls. But for most of the decade the NSA and the FBI strongly opposed lifting them. While the issue of export controls might seem arcane, it had important implications for encryption in the United States. Computer manufacturers balked at having to offer two separate products, one with weakened security for the export market and another with stronger security for domestic markets, and so products with the weaker security won. Thus the export controls effectively limited domestic use of encryption technologies.

Cryptography enables the confidential transmission of communications, such as that of a credit card number from a customer's computer to a website. Cryptography facilitates the process of authenticating communications, assuring one party that the other is who she claims to be. This is essential: for a customer to shop in confidence, for instance, she must be sure that she really is communicating with Amazon. And cryptography assists in integrity checking, that is, protecting the message against tampering while in transit. The export-control rules were confusing; they restricted exporting cryptography when it was used for confidentiality, but allowed it if it was used for authentication or integrity checking. Sometimes the authorities imposed restrictions on permitted exceptions, despite the fact that the regulations allowed them.

Another push to remove the controls came from the US Department of Defense, which increasingly relied on Silicon Valley for new technology. In part, this decision was driven by cost: modified commercial off-the-shelf systems cost considerably less than custom-designed models. In part, it was due to speed: entrepreneurs innovated for the private market at many times the speed they could innovate for the Pentagon. But to a certain extent, the military's partnership with Silicon Valley emerged from the changing nature of US alliances. Sharing cryptographic technologies with long-term allies is one thing, but doing so with ad hoc coalition partners, such as those of the First Gulf War, is quite another. This year's coalition may very well contain next year's opponents. A secure commercial off-the-shelf system offers all the benefits of secure communications without the risk that sharing classified systems would.

In response to these pressures, in 2000 the White House lifted export controls on computer and communications devices with strong cryptography, so long as the equipment wasn't going to a communications provider or a government, and wasn't custom-built. This solution pleased manufacturers: the consumer equipment they were interested in exporting was no longer controlled. And it satisfied NSA, for controls remained in place for exactly the type of equipment most of interest to the signals-intelligence agency (signals intelligence consists of gathering information from intercepting communications and other electronic signals).

The solution did not please the FBI, however, and it quickly began fighting back. Its tool of choice was the Communications Assistance for Law Enforcement Act (CALEA), passed by Congress in 1994. This law required that digital telephone networks—which is to say, all modern telephone networks—have wiretapping capabilities built into the phone switches. The law exempted the then-nascent Internet from similar requirements.

If the idea of putting an interception back door in a phone switch—that is, with wiretapping capabilities just waiting to be turned on—sounds insecure, that intuition is correct. Such a model invites hackers, and yes, hackers soon accepted the invitation. The most famous case is that of Vodafone Greece, the Greek subsidiary of the telecommunications company. Hackers attacked a switch that had been built to comply with European requirements that mimicked CALEA. For ten months between 2004 and 2005, one hundred senior members of the Greek government, including the prime minister, were wiretapped by unknown parties. But this is hardly the only instance of backdoor wiretapping capabilities creating security problems. In the mid-2000s, for example, when the NSA tested CALEA-compliant phone switches for possible use by the US military, the agency discovered that every single one had a security flaw.[11]

Despite the security problems CALEA was creating, the FBI pressed to extend the law to the Internet. The bureau succeeded in 2005 in extending the law to cover some cases of

Voice over Internet Protocol (VoIP) communications. In 2010, the FBI stepped up its demands. Claiming that law enforcement was "going dark" because of complexities introduced by modern communications—including encryption and a constant introduction of new Internet applications—the FBI pressed for changes in the law. The bureau wanted any form of encryption to have some form of "exceptional access" so that law enforcement could wiretap when it had a proper court order. The FBI also sought to require manufacturers to design phones so that they could be searched when there was a proper court order.[12]

Without question, encryption—of communications, of the data on phones—makes law enforcement's job more difficult. Investigators particularly rely on wiretapping to investigate those crimes that leave no immediate evidence—no dead bodies, no obvious thefts, broken windows, or wrecked cars. Some cases leave no physical evidence at all: bribery and corruption fall into this category.

Consider the example of insider trading—the trading of stocks or other securities by those with access to nonpublic information. Many nations with advanced economies have laws against insider trading; the US is particularly strict on this issue, and puts great emphasis on enforcement. Recently, US prosecutors have intensified their pursuit of insider trading violations. Some, including the former US attorney for the Southern District of New York, Preet Bharara, had made such cases a prime focus of their work.[13]

Because even determining that such a conspiracy has occurred is difficult, investigators have turned to electronic eavesdropping. But US laws on wiretapping are strict, and in criminal cases investigators must demonstrate probable cause before being allowed to wiretap within the United States. The tried-and-true way to investigate conspiracies, be it corruption, insider trading, or organized crime, is to garner evidence on a low-level player, and then use the threat of jail to coerce the suspect into obtaining evidence against an individual higher up the chain. Then repeat. That's what government investigators did here.

In 2007, the Securities and Exchange Commission (SEC) received an anonymous letter suggesting that the Galleon Group, a hedge fund, was engaged in insider trading. But the letter provided no specific details to help investigators pull apart the ball of wool. The government started its investigation by interviewing Raj Rajaratnam, Galleon's head. Just before an afternoon break, asking a seemingly offhand question, the government investigators queried Rajaratnam about some instant messages he had received from someone identified as roomy81. The instant messages suggested that the writer was providing Rajaratnam with insider information about Polycom, a communications technology company. "She worked at Galleon," Rajaratnam responded—and he gave investigators roomy81's name, Roomy Khan.[14]

Law enforcement began digging. The FBI discovered that Khan had supplied valuable inside information to Rajaratnam on Hilton, Intel, Google, and a number of other companies. Two FBI special agents went to Khan's house with a file documenting her illegal communications with Rajaratnam. The evidence worked as expected; to escape a jail sentence, Khan cooperated with the investigation and taped calls with Rajaratnam. This new evidence enabled investigators to get a wiretap order directly on Rajaratnam. In the end, forty-seven people were charged with insider trading; by 2011, thirty-five of them had been convicted. In large part, prosecutors owed their success to the wiretap. Rajaratnam received an eleven-year jail sentence, the longest sentence ever received for insider trading.[15]

In other cases, investigators may not need to know the actual content of a call. Cellphones provide all sorts of interesting information, especially about a user's location. In order to connect calls, cellphones must constantly notify cell towers of their location, effectively saying, "Here I am." These notifications—the phone's location at a particular time—occur regardless of whether a conversation is taking place. By providing location, cellphones vastly simplify investigations. Sometimes, this phone metadata is even more valuable than the content.

On July 7, 2005, London experienced a terrorist attack. Four suicide bombers attacked the London transit system, blowing themselves up on three Underground cars and one bus. The bombings killed fifty-two people and injured more than 700, making it the worst terrorist attack in Britain in over thirty years.

Two weeks later, on July 21, four men who had been preparing bombs independently of the July 7 group attempted a similar attack. This time the bombs—placed at three London Underground stations and on one bus—failed to properly detonate. The original detonation in each bomb worked, producing smoke and noise. But in each case, the larger detonator failed, and there were only minimal explosions. At this point police were unsure of what, exactly, they were looking at; the bombs were similar in design to those that had exploded on July 7, but they had failed. Two days later, an abandoned bomb was found in a London park.

None of the second set of would-be bombers were caught at the scene. But the closed-circuit television (CCTV) cameras that are ubiquitous in the United Kingdom caught images of each bomber. A day after the attempted bombings, police released photos of the four suspects. Within an hour the father of one of the suspects called police and provided names for two of them: Yassin Hassan Omar and Muktar Said Ibrahim.[16]

In video footage taken at a London bus station, six-foot-tall Omar is wearing a burka. No one had noticed him as he fled by bus to Birmingham. But Omar didn't wear the burka as he moved around Birmingham, and that was his undoing. Within four days, a Birmingham resident reported Omar to the police, and he was arrested early the next morning. Authorities caught up with Ibrahim and another would-be bomber, Ramzi Mohammed, on July 29 after a neighbor recognized Ibrahim from a police photo and tipped off the police.[17]

The fourth suspect, recognized by a neighbor from a CCTV photo taken shortly before the attempted bombing, managed to flee the country. After his bomb failed to explode in the subway car at the Shepherd's Bush station, Hussain Osman fled across the tracks, onto the streets, and through the front door and out the back of someone's home. At some point, he called his wife, who picked him up and drove him to Brighton, where he hid for two days. Osman then returned to London and traveled to Rome. And here is where modern communications systems tripped him up.[18]

Osman fled to Italy on his brother's passport. But he used a phone from his brother-in-law, and British and Italian law enforcement tracked it. They followed the signal four days after the attacks at Waterloo Station in London, then found it in Paris two days later, and in Milan and Bologna a day later. The next morning the phone was used in the Rome neighborhood where Osman's brother lived. Police captured Osman later that day. Law enforcement never listened to the call content; the phone signal alone had given Osman's location away.[19]

Sometimes, though, government does need to be able to access communications content. But increasing cyberthreats have put the communications of individuals and corporations at risk as well.

The 2014 attack on Sony Pictures is a case in point. Until quite recently, the film industry's main product—the film itself —was a physical object that was shipped in metal canisters to movie theaters and shipped back after theatrical release. Now films are bits, shipped electronically—and stolen electronically. Sony Pictures is in the bits business, something the company seems to have understood somewhat too late.

On November 24, 2014, the Sony studio heads received a threatening email that read, "We've obtained all your internal data including your secrets and top secrets. If you don't obey us, we'll release data shown below to the world." This was the Monday before Thanksgiving. At the same time, a "screen of death"—a skeleton superimposed on the above message— appeared on every computer on the Sony Pictures Entertainment worldwide network.[20]

Unbeknownst to its executives, Sony had experienced a massive data breach. The attackers had gained an intimate knowledge not only of the content of Sony's computer systems, but also of the best ways to traverse them. They knew which machines controlled which others and how data flowed within the system. They had user names and passwords to the routers and switches within the system. They knew the details for the RSA SecureID tokens used to authenticate users and systems. In short, they knew virtually everything there was to know about how the Sony system was secured.[21]

The attackers—a group calling themselves "Guardians of Peace"—had stolen five unreleased Sony pictures and a script to a James Bond movie in development. The attackers also published internal emails, which embarrassed a number of Sony

producers and actors, and loaded stolen movies onto illegal
file-sharing sites. Sony's IT department discovered that the internal data centers had had their data wiped; more than 3,000
computers and 800 Sony servers were destroyed because the
attackers killed the machines' startup software.[22]

In response, Sony moved into a 1990s mode of operation. The company shut down its remaining computers, and
executives dusted off their old, disused BlackBerrys. Employees set up phone trees.[23]

Soon the attack moved from the realm of private property to physical threats. On December 8, Sony received a demand to immediately stop distribution of *The Interview*, a
comedy mocking North Korea's leader Kim Jong-un. On December 16, the threats escalated, hinting at attacks at theaters
showing the film.

The FBI, meanwhile, announced that North Korea was
behind the attack. That made attacks at movie theaters highly
unlikely. Launching a cyberattack against a company's servers
from across the Pacific is one thing; mounting physical attacks
on US movie theaters is another thing entirely. But as theaters
began canceling screenings, Sony halted the film's distribution.
President Obama stepped in, urging Sony to show some back-
bone: "Do not get into a pattern in which you're intimidated
by these kinds of criminal attacks." Confirming that North
Korea was the attacker, the president said that United States
would respond proportionally in a place, time, and manner of
its own choice.[24]

Sony ultimately showed the film, making over $40 mil-
lion on it within the first month—far less than what the North
Korean attack had cost the company. The real issue, however—
the one President Obama alluded to—was that a nation-state
had used cyberspace to threaten and disrupt activities beyond

its shores. At first, some researchers in the security community doubted that the United States had proof of North Korea's involvement in the attacks; Edward Snowden's disclosures on the NSA's activities convinced doubters that it did.[25]

The Sony affair was not the first instance of a state-sponsored attack against a corporation. Iran apparently responded to the 2009 cyberattack on its nuclear centrifuges (discussed in Chapter 3) by launching a cyberattack on a Saudi oil company, Aramco, and destroying three-quarters of the company's PCs. One can view Iran's attack as hurling a brick back at a neighbor's house after its own windows had been broken. North Korea's action, on the other hand, was a serious escalation of cyberattacks for relatively trivial issues. As such things go, the attack against Sony was not particularly sophisticated. "Spear phishing" emails—targeted emails with links to infected files—sent to Sony employees enabled attackers to access Sony's network. When users clicked on the links, the attackers gained the ability to conduct reconnaissance on the Sony systems. They learned account names, user names, and passwords. Sony's accounts, including those for system administrators—people who have access to all the internal Sony systems—did not employ strong forms of authentication. Instead, Sony relied on passwords.[26]

This was an exceptionally poor idea. Passwords are easy to steal or even guess, and security systems don't usually notice the theft until someone attempts to use the password. Sony should have been using a stronger form of authentication.

Multifactor authentication can be done in various ways. Gmail users, for example, receive a onetime code either via SMS text from Google or from an app on their phones. Alternate technologies enable a user to log in by simply tapping a notification on their phone.

Mobile phones provide an excellent way of securely authenticating an account. That's because people always have their phones with them, and the user knows if the phone has gone missing. In order to remotely log in, hackers would need to have not only passwords but the information provided by the phones. Stealing ten dozen passwords—or even ten thousand —can be done stealthily. Stealing even a half dozen phones is much less easily accomplished; stealing them so that the theft is not discovered until the hack occurs is close to impossible. Because phone authentication systems have been designed to be easy to use, people actually use them, rather than trying to find ways to evade the technology.

A number of companies already employ smartphone multifactor authentication. Prior to the North Korean attack, Sony did not. Sony's executives had not fully understood that the company was in the business of producing bits—and that therefore their business depended on securing those bits just as much as a bank must protect its cash (which is *also* stored as bits). Instead of storing its email indefinitely and allowing employees easy access to online information, Sony archives emails for only a few weeks, and the company moved certain information so that it was no longer accessible from the Internet; that lack of convenience carries its own cost, of course. (Sony has not revealed whether these security measures include multifactor authentication for email access.) While Sony learned its lesson, many others in the private sector remained far too unconcerned about the risks of a cyberattack against their company's assets.[27]

One can argue about whether North Korea's attack on Sony constituted a national security issue, but no such ambiguity surrounds an attack on the Ukrainian power grid. Late on the afternoon of December 23, 2015, the control centers of three power distribution companies in western Ukraine were attacked within thirty minutes of each other. Hackers disconnected at least twenty-seven substations, shutting off power to about 225 million customers for one to six hours. The attackers "bricked" devices that would have allowed operators to bring substations back through online tools and wiped out workstations and servers. All this made recovery much more difficult. The attackers took control of operators' workstations and disabled backup power supplies to two of the distribution centers, leaving operators working both literally and figuratively in the dark.[28]

The attack began in much the same way as the North Korean cyberattack against Sony. Someone sent company workers spear-phishing emails, this time with malicious Microsoft Office attachments. By opening the attachments, the recipients granted the hackers access to the business networks of the Ukrainian power distribution companies. Just as with the Sony cyberattack, the attackers used this initial access to conduct reconnaissance of the business networks. The attackers removed information and, most devastatingly, collected login credentials to various systems.[29]

There are various computer networks used by power distribution companies. The business network manages customer accounts, payroll, and the like. The control network manages the power grid, sending messages to open and close breakers, enabling power to flow. An operator on this network can open and shut breakers at power substations. All three power distribution centers used simple passwords to authenticate system operators; it was these credentials that the hackers stole.

Once in the systems, the North Korean attack on Sony and the attack on the Ukrainian power grid differed markedly in technical sophistication. The North Korean attack used well-known tools and was not customized. By contrast, the attack on the Ukrainian power grid employed tools that had been tailored to the individual control systems of each of the three distribution companies. From the clockwork ease by which the attack proceeded, it appears that the attackers had tested the tools to see if they worked. They did so in a system within their own organization; this organization had substantial technical resources.[30]

In a successful effort to upset the grid customers, the attackers prevented them from calling in to report on the outage. They did this through a "telephone denial-of-service" attack. When power went down, the companies' call centers were flooded with calls. But the thousands of calls were apparently from Moscow, not western Ukraine, the site of the outage. Denial-of-service, an attack that so overloads the system that regular users can't get through, is common. At moments when connectivity is crucial, such attacks can be devastating. In this case, though, the telephone denial-of-service was just another annoyance to frustrated customers. That was undoubtedly its purpose.[31]

This attack on the Ukrainian power grid was preventable. A defensive system would have started with strong authentication systems. The system should have monitored the internal network, grid control devices, and outgoing traffic for abnormal behavior. The best system of protection in this case would have sharply limited remote access. The Ukrainian power grid system appears not to have taken any of these protective steps.[32]

Instead, employees of the three Ukrainian distribution companies—the networks that had been penetrated when users originally opened the corrupt attachments—could access the control networks without using multifactor authentication. And thus so could the attackers. Trading security for convenience opened the Ukrainian power grid to a potentially devastating attack. But the Ukrainian power grid still had manual controls, which made bringing systems back up easier than if they had all been automated. The attacks nonetheless sent a chilling message: we can get into your critical infrastructure networks, and we can bring them down. The attack was conducted against Ukraine, but the message may well have been intended for other nations.[33]

We live in a highly interconnected world. The electronic tools that society and individuals have come to rely on, such as cellphones, provide sufficient information to identify a would-be bomber or convict an inside trader. Similarly, the connectivity and remote access that enable companies to ship products digitally and operators to control large, complex systems at a distance can allow attackers to reach inside an organization and steal and manipulate its data.

We live in an age of insecurity. Terrorists select their targets not only from the list of expected places, but also apparently at random: a holiday celebration at work, a gay nightclub, a sidewalk after Bastille Day fireworks. Terrorists intend that apparent randomness to create additional horror. Our societal response, so far, has been to demand that government do everything it can to keep us safe. But safety has many components, and keeping us secure requires thinking carefully and rationally about sources of risk.

This includes cybersecurity. What are the costs of designing systems so that listening in is always possible? How do the calculations of risk change when cyberattacks and cyberexploitation are deeply serious threats? Only by understanding these risks can we make sound choices regarding encryption.

2

We're All Connected Now

The notion that institutions might flourish through greater connectivity—faster access to knowledge, easier collaborations across institutions—caught on quickly in the 1990s. When a network is fast enough, you don't even need to host computational power on your own machine. That's the idea behind cloud computing, where users send out their computations to a provider who performs the operations and returns the results to the user. To the public, Amazon is an e-commerce company, a seller of everything from books to wine. But to the computer industry, Amazon is a cloud company, with Amazon Web Services (AWS) providing processing power and memory on demand. AWS is like a utility that sells computing cycles rather than water or electricity. Cloud services are particularly useful for startups, which may grow faster than their computing resources. Even companies one would never anticipate needing massive computation avail themselves of the cloud. Etsy, for instance, uses cloud computing to analyze user actions and determine better ways to provide customers with the products they want. But small companies are not the only organizations to rely on cloud computing. Large organizations, including the US government, do as well.[1]

Distributed computing, in which a single complex computation is broken down into many pieces that are done on disparate machines and then recombined, is another way of using the network to compute. Want to help medical researchers without lifting a finger? Join the Rosetta@home project, which harnesses the power of 60,000 volunteers' idling computers to model how different proteins connect with each other and to design new proteins. In November 2016 the donated computing power averaged out to 120 teraFlops (that's equivalent to having about 60,000 dedicated workstations). If you prefer decrypting World War II messages or searching for pulsars, researchers would also welcome your help.[2]

Network communication is cheap and ever more widely available. Between 2011 and 2016, international bandwidth quadrupled; so did usage. The Internet opened to commercial traffic in 1995. By December of that year, 16 million people were using the network. Growth was spectacular, for a while doubling each year. As I write these words in the fall of 2016, approximately 3.6 billion people use the Internet. But traditional computers no longer represent the fastest source of growth. Instead, Internet expansion is fueled by devices, the so-called Internet of Things (IoT).[3]

The growth is driven by sensors, devices that simply measure data. Sensors—for instance, thermometers—have existed for a long time. Now they are cheap, which means they are everywhere. All new cars sold in the United States after 2008 have tire-pressure sensors; a dashboard light goes on to signal an underinflated tire. Bridges are being fitted with vibration sensors to monitor stability. Smartphones are filled with sensors: accelerometers and gyroscopes to determine the orientation of the phone and adjust the screen accordingly, light sensors that check on ambient brightness to save battery power by adjusting the screen, magnetic field sensors to enable the phone to act as a compass, and thermometers to measure the phone's temperature. All this sensor data is being collected, indexed, and used—and increasingly finding its way to the Internet. Sensors measure the lubrication of a machine tool, the humidity of the soil, the color of a leaf, a wearer's pulse rate and blood glucose levels. Collecting and connecting this data is changing the way we live and work.

The Digital Revolution has changed our society in profound ways, and it has changed the risks we face. Where once we produced goods, now a great proportion of production is intellectual property—the ideas and designs for these goods. And the plans for computer systems, wind turbines, new pharmaceuticals, and the like are far more mobile than the objects themselves—and often more valuable.

All kinds of data are important for economic competitiveness and national security. Who, for instance, would have thought that crop data matters? But in 1972, by intercepting communications between US farmers and the Department of Agriculture, the Soviet Union knew more about prices and crop status than the US government did. The Soviet Union used this information to buy $750 million dollars' worth of American grain at subsidized prices. A year later, wheat prices around the world jumped by 200 to 350 percent, and everyone realized that the Soviet Union had gotten itself a very good deal.[4]

The Digital Revolution's networks have raised the stakes of information. In 2015, for instance, someone stole 80 million healthcare records from the insurance giant Anthem/Blue Cross. This information likely ended up in the hands of criminals who could use it to commit identity theft or medical fraud. To understand the risks our society faces, we must start by looking at how the Digital Revolution is embedding itself into our lives.

The Industrial Revolution had two phases: mechanizing the manufacturing of cloth, then mechanizing manufacturing itself. The Digital Revolution is experiencing the same two-step process. In the first phase, the white-collar side of industry—payroll, human resources, inventory management—was digitized and networked. Computers have been used to design complex industrial parts for decades. We're now entering the second phase of the Digital Revolution, one in which we're networking the production processes themselves.

Monitoring and networking are greatly increasing efficiency on the factory floor. Machines that make machines—machine tools, in engineering parlance—are industry's workhorses; they make everything from microswitches to the pylons that transport research vehicles underneath the wings of NASA's B-52 plane. Depending on its size and complexity, a machine tool costs between several thousand and several million dollars. Running them efficiently is key to productivity.[5]

Machine tools have been computer-controlled since the 1950s, and sensors enable the tools to work extraordinarily precisely. But sensors can do much more than this. They can tell if the orientation of the cutter has shifted, if a part needs lubrication, or whether a tool's vibration has increased (which could ruin the parts the tool is cutting). Sensors can also report on how efficiently the tool is working. If asked, most plant managers will tell you that the machine tools in their plants operate two-thirds to three-quarters of the time the plant is functioning. But automatic reporting from sensors shows that factories usually operate about half that. Networking the full factory floor is extremely useful; it gives plant managers highly accurate, up-to-the-minute data on part production, asset utilization, machine health, energy use, and more. Such simple changes as introducing electronic dashboards showing machine availability and efficiency can increase productivity by 20 percent.[6]

A fully networked plant enables manufacturers to take advantage of other kinds of services. Some of these provide extraordinary value. A Japanese company, FANUC, makes large industrial robots that are amazing to watch. These million-dollar machines perform highly complex jobs such as assembling cars, and they do so with great efficiency. But their efficiency is their Achilles' heel; when a robot unexpectedly goes offline, the company using the robots wastes thousands of dollars a minute in lost production time. Catching problems early, before a robot needs a more serious repair, is key. But how to do it?

FANUC approached the problem by asking Cisco, the information technology company, to come up with a way for the robots to securely report data from sensors to several different recipients, both human and robot, in various locations. When a sensor indicates that a robot is experiencing an increasing level of resistance, for example, smartphone alerts go to everyone in the robot's contact list (you didn't know a robot had a contact list, did you?). Service centers at both the manufacturing company and FANUC are informed; FANUC analyzes and diagnoses the problem—and might even ship out a replacement part. If FANUC gets a series of messages indicating similar problems at different sites, the robot company might start investigating the possibility of a systemic problem with the equipment.[7]

The combination of reporting and data analysis enables FANUC to alert its customers to upcoming preventative maintenance issues. Rick Schneider, CEO of FANUC's American division, says that the system allows the company to predict instead of react. Within six months of having its robots networked, an automotive company estimated it had saved $40 million by preventing downtime. Or as Cisco has named the project: Zero Downtime.[8]

The ability to network and monitor machines from afar is changing how manufacturers make and market their products. GE, that mainstay of American manufacturing, produces wind turbines and jet engines along with the more familiar light bulbs and refrigerators. It used to be that GE sold jet engines and locomotives. These days the company promises a certain level of thrust and locomotion from the machine. If it doesn't deliver, GE pays a penalty. So the company is installing sensors and measuring everything it can to deliver performance.[9]

If that sounds to you like the Digital Revolution approach to industry, you're correct. Each day, each pair of engines on the Boeing 787 Dreamliner ships a terabyte of data back to GE, which now has a plant in Silicon Valley. GE is learning how to employ Big Data to improve the efficiency and reliability of its products. In one case GE observed that the company's jet engines being used in the Middle East and China needed maintenance more frequently than engines used elsewhere; analysis of the sensor information showed the engines were clogging more often. Now those engines are cleaned more frequently than those in the United States; the clogging problem went away.[10]

Many other companies are taking similar approaches to providing their customers with products that function more efficiently, and with less down time. Bits are increasingly used to monitor and control the physical processes of manufacturing,

the making of plane struts, car doors, microswitches, wind turbines, smartphone cases, and pretty much everything else.

Even farmers are relying on bits to manage their work. It used
to be that the most reliable way to learn what crop grew well in
a field was to ask the farmer. Now you might as well ask a computer. Different parts of a field have different profiles, with varying pH levels in the soil, pest infestations, and drainage. These
all affect how crops grow. Maximizing yield means taking advantage of such information. What's the best way to do it? Put
sensors in the field and sensors on the farm equipment. Field
sensors measure soil humidity and tell the farmer when and
where to water. Drone-based sensors can tell farmers when their
crops are at their prime to harvest. Equipment sensors measure
the crop's moisture as it is harvested as well as in the grain bin.
Excess moisture means a lower price for crops, so some farmers
need to dry their harvest at home, but overdrying wastes expensive fuel. Automatic moisture sensors help a farmer decide when
to turn off the fan and when to haul the crops to market.

The cab of a contemporary combine harvester is filled
with computer screens. Sensors throughout the combine monitor grain loss, bushels harvested per hour, optimum clearance,
and yield per acre. Plugged-in farmers can use this information to create a map and prescription for next year's fertilizer
order, hybrid selection, and herbicide needs. There's also a steering wheel, but better steering is often accomplished through
GPS or mechanical sensors that actually feel the crop. Farm
fields are not perfect rectangles; they have bumps, dips, wet
spots, trees and other obstacles, and the combine can be easily
programmed to follow rows more accurately than can human
drivers. But GPS does much more than that for farmers. For
example, GPS guidance ensures that, as a farmer sprays herbi-

cide in adjacent fields, plants on the edges of fields receive only one application, not two. That's good for the environment and operating costs.

Other sensors in harvesting equipment guide other actions. Different crops require different cutting heights; these matter. In sugar cane, for example, the best sugar is in the bottom half inch of the cane. But cutting closer than a tenth of an inch from the ground collects dirt along with the cane. Soybeans are another example: plants up to four feet tall have pods as low as two inches from the ground;. Again, sensors position the harvester correctly. Other sensors automatically guide the optimal filling of grain trailers. In much the way they work on the factory floor, machine sensors also monitor the state of the equipment. Running tractors and combines efficiently matters, so it should be no surprise that the machinery is carefully instrumented in order to ensure that happens. Sensors measure engine load, for example, and the machine's computers are constantly calculating the most efficient use of fuel.

Sensors aren't only in the fields, on the plants, and on farm equipment—they are also on the animals. Cows won't tell us how they are feeling, but sensors can provide some insight. A cow's movement and temperature are useful indicators that she's ready for breeding or coming down with mastitis (the most common disease of dairy cows). Though farming will always be part of the physical world, more and more of its management is being done through the world of bits.[11]

Our own health is also being transformed by insights derived from bits. Better data will help us understand the causes and treatments of disease. With sensors and networking, we can collect and analyze data even at the level of an individual. Certainly, such data is subject to odd individual variations, but combining data from sensors enables us to build a more complex understanding of how diseases present and progress on a population level.

Networked health monitoring systems are already improving the health and quality of life for people with chronic conditions. People with diabetes, for instance, can use under-the-skin sensors to continually monitor their glucose levels. This approach allows individuals and their doctors to hone treatments; with education and practice, patients can learn to adjust their medication levels at home. Were the person a machine tool, we'd call the sensors and monitoring preventative maintenance. Similar tools can be used to monitor blood pressure, mobility, and seizure activity.[12]

Working with TigerPlace, an assisted living community that functions as a "living laboratory" in Columbia, Missouri, University of Missouri researchers experimented with sensors to improve the quality of life for geriatric patients. The elderly present a challenge to doctors. Older people take longer to recover from treatment than young people; this is especially true of bed stays, where the elderly lose strength quickly. Catching and treating problems early is especially important for the elderly. Sensors can measure changes long before people themselves are really aware of problems. Researchers wondered: could sensors help in early intervention?

To find out, they deployed a set of sensors in the rooms of some residents at TigerPlace. Motion sensors captured daytime movement, and bed sensors measured bedtime restlessness, pulse, and breathing. When a patient exhibited a notable change in behavior, the devices alerted the nursing staff, who then intervened as appropriate. The technology proved valuable. After a year, hand-grip strength, a predictor of frailty and mortality, was noticeably greater in the group living with sensors. So was gait quality. It was a small experiment—forty-two people in all—so the results can hardly be considered definitive. But to the staff at TigerPlace, the point had been validated. The community now encourages all residents to have sensors installed.[13]

Some researchers are intrigued by the possibility of using similar tools for personalized medical treatment. Parkinson's disease affects muscles and speech, progressively causing tremors, rigidity, impaired movement, and slowed speech, among other symptoms. The disease's trajectory, however, varies widely from patient to patient. Patients typically see their doctors only every four to six months, too infrequently to track daily changes. Given the nature of the illness, doctors find it challenging to gain an intimate understanding of how a patient's situation is changing. An effortless way to get a rich source of data about patients is to collect information from a device they always have with them. Apple's ResearchKit turns an iPhone into a collector of medical data. Over 9,000 people enrolled in a study conducted by researchers at Sage Bionetworks and the University of Rochester that used iPhones to test patients' memory, finger dexterity, and speed, and recorded voice, gait, and balance three times daily. This type of detailed reporting may ultimately not only improve our understanding of Parkinson's disease, but may also enable doctors to individualize treatment plans for patients with this difficult disease.[14]

Using sensors, smartphones, monitoring, and networking, healthcare—not costs, but actual care—is becoming a data-driven, bits-controlled system. Sensors are transforming how we manufacture, farm, and manage our health. They can play this role because the underlying communications infrastructure —the Internet—has reached a speed that enables users to aggregate, analyze, and act on data gathered in near-real time by sensors. Sensors and connectivity are changing the future.

The Internet has already changed our present. While each of us might rank the changes engendered by the Digital Revolution differently, its impact on critical infrastructure has to be close to the top.

The very existence of critical infrastructure is a consequence of the original Industrial Revolution. Telecommunications, transportation infrastructure, electricity, modern water supplies, banks, and financial systems are both products of modern society and crucial enablers of it. These underpinnings often started out small and local, but efficiencies of scale led to larger networks. Systems that move goods—whether those goods are voices, bits, people, materials, food, or money—are simply more efficient when they're larger. A telephone that only connects to a few other phones offers little value for its users. And transportation infrastructure—roads, railways, and canals —clearly needs to connect to fulfill its basic purpose.[15]

Electric power seemed to be an exception to this rule, at least in the beginning. Because energy is lost when electricity travels, early users of electricity relied on nearby generators. This worked fine in the nineteenth century, when manufacturers and consumers used relatively little electrical power. But rapid industrialization increased demand for power in the early twentieth century, as did the later widespread adoption of the conveniences of modern life (refrigerators, TVs, washing machines, air conditioners, microwaves). Interconnecting adjacent power systems let suppliers obtain excess power for distribution from neighboring facilities at less than the cost of building a new power plant. By the middle of the twentieth century, these networks expanded, and the electrical distribution system had consolidated. Where power generation once consisted of small networks that provided electricity to a single factory or small town, by the 1960s US power grid transmission systems had become highly interconnected and geographically distributed.[16]

Even in this interconnected system, however, the United States relies on a diverse set of electrical suppliers. Some of these suppliers, like the Tennessee Valley Authority, are publicly owned. Some small ones are owned by rural cooperatives. Large suppliers may serve many millions of customers, while small ones may serve only a few thousand (Holyoke Gas and Electric in western Massachusetts, for instance, has 17,000 customers). Some systems only supply power, while others both generate and distribute power. The North American system—US and Canadian power supplies are interconnected—consists of two major (eastern and western) and three minor power grids (Quebec, Texas, and Alaska). Each system consists of high-voltage transmission grids that connect generating systems to the power distribution system; the distribution system, which "steps down" the power to a lower voltage to deliver it to consumers; and an operations system that manages these interconnections.[17]

The power distribution system worked reasonably well for decades. But a 1965 blackout that left 30 million people in the northeastern United States and eastern Canada in the dark for thirteen hours served as the first warning of the risks of such a large system. Lights went out from Manhattan to northern Ontario and Quebec. An Ontario safety relay, incorrectly set, tripped, creating a cascading system overload.

In systems as large as the North American grids, local failures can quickly cascade into a regional crisis. Systems had to be designed so that failing components could be quickly identified and isolated. The lesson was not learned as well as it might have been: in August 2003, a cascading failure shut off power to 50 million people across the Midwest and northeastern

United States, as well as in southeastern Canada. By the beginning of the twenty-first century, power transmission systems had become even more highly interconnected—and very complex.[18]

Recent regulatory changes have added to the power system's complexity. Companies now compete with one another to offer lower-cost electricity to consumers. With deregulation, states loosened their controls on prices companies could charge consumers. Thus a power supplier's calculation as to whether it should produce its own power, or distribute someone else's, became more complex. The people in charge of making these decisions need immediate access to information about both their suppliers and their competitors. What is the going price for a kilowatt hour, right now? The smart grid, which may shut off or slow down appliances during times of high energy use, is adding yet another set of control requirements. Energy producers who rely on renewable resources, like wind and solar power, face the additional complication of variable supply.

In one sense, the electrical system quite literally consists of atoms—electrical current is the movement of electrons along a conductor, usually a wire. When hackers disrupted the computer control systems that ran the Ukrainian power grid, system operators turned the power back on by hand, using manual controls. This may no longer be possible in the United States, where the electrical system has been modernized to the point that it is almost entirely managed by computer networks—that is, bits. It might take operators in the United States much longer than six hours to respond if a similar attack occurred within North America.

The modern financial system, based on electronic transfers and credit cards, is part of critical infrastructure. Modern societies rely on the easy flow of money to purchase services from afar. Liquidity allows trade; without it, goods cease to flow. Indeed, the US government views banking and the financial system as "central to the functioning of commerce and the daily lives of Americans."[19]

Like power generation, banks were originally local. In many places, they still are. This made sense when trade moved at the pace of a ship or a train; bankers could send telegrams in an emergency. Through the mid-1970s, banks used a remote communications technology called telex that delivered text messages over telephone lines, with the message printed out at the other end. But telex was slow and insecure, and, as banks consolidated, first regionally and then nationally, they looked for better ways to communicate.

In 1973 a consortium of banks set up the Society for Worldwide Interbank Financial Telecommunication (SWIFT). SWIFT provides an efficient and secure messaging system for interbank payment orders. The banks themselves do the crucial work of transferring funds and processing payments; SWIFT just transmits the messages. Transmission is in bits, of course.

SWIFT communications are encrypted. In banking, however, the need for confidentiality ranks second in importance to ensuring the message's authenticity and integrity. When financial institutions communicate, they need to know that they are talking with the correct party; thus authentication is critical for both the sender and receiver. And the transmission itself must be accurate. A zero in the wrong place can mean the difference between transferring 10 million pounds and transferring 100 million. Banks record these transactions and make them available to auditors because their own financial integrity depends on being able to correct errors. Banking is a highly regulated industry, and bank records are available to governments under the relevant legal authorities (countries vary on this, of course). To prevent money laundering, US law, for example, requires banks to report cash transactions of over $10,000.

Since the 1970s, banks and other financial institutions have relied on SWIFT for their electronic payment order messages. But until quite recently, electronic transactions were the exception rather than the rule. People have relied on cash, or other tangible forms of wealth, for millennia. Paying by cash carries its own set of risks. Money has to be transported from the bank to the merchant and from the merchant to the bank; it has to be counted when it's received, counted at the end of the day, and counted when it is deposited. Merchants have to make sure no one is stealing from the register; individuals have to guard their wallets.

Cash payments are ebbing. Instead of buying subway tokens with cash, or peeling off a few bills to pick up the dry cleaning, consumers increasingly pay with some kind of virtual money, such as credit or debit cards (checks appear to be going the way of the dinosaur). Contactless cards, such as those used by many mass transit systems, smartphone payment systems, and networked tablets (such as iPads) have made paying electronically simpler and faster than it once was—and often easier than cash. And merchants prefer electronic payments; they are efficient and cut down on security issues. Banks and other financial institutions prefer them, too, because they get a small cut on each payment. Increasingly, certain types of transactions—public transport, highway tolls, parking garages— require electronic payment.[20]

For all its inconvenience, cash offers certain advantages —especially for privacy. Cash payments leave no trail. Cash packs easily: a million dollars can be packed inside a shopping bag or small suitcase. It's much safer for a drug dealer to move his profits in bundles than by trying a risky electronic funds transfer, which will leave a trail. The underground economy thrives on cash. Muggers especially like (other people's) cash.

Governments prefer bits. Electronic money is traceable, making it much less useful for the underground economy and bribes (a major reason India suddenly withdrew 500 and 1,000 rupee notes from circulation, a step that may move the nation toward a cashless society). Robberies and muggings decrease in a cashless society. Of course, going cashless creates problems, not just for those who can't get credit cards, but also for privacy. Now there's a record of each time you pick up a pack of cigarettes.[21]

Swedish banks have made a cashless society easy; they developed a smartphone app that allows simple peer-to-peer payments. In Sweden, less than 2 percent of transactions counted in the gross domestic product are in cash. Beggars in Stockholm accept contributions in plastic (charities have handed out card readers). Denmark, Norway, and Belgium are following Sweden's lead and moving away from cash. And the same conversation has even begun to arise in India.[22]

In a matter of several decades, almost every aspect of how we interact with the world has changed in fundamental ways. We may still cook, eat, go for a run, make love, have children, diaper babies, and care for elderly parents, but our interactions with the physical world are increasingly mediated by bits. The change happened because data networks are growing faster and cheaper, sensors are dropping in price, and ever more data, mostly in bits, is becoming available. Together, these changes have enabled four new ways of interacting with the world: we can substitute artifacts for real objects, easily run experiments, work at scale, and control processes at a distance. Let me explain each of these.

We use bits as artifacts, to stand in for the real thing. Google Maps finds out about traffic congestion not by sending cars out to watch the roads, nor by using drones to take pictures. Instead, Google "crowdsources" traffic data from users of their products who may not even realize they're supplying information. Let's say a driver has Google Maps installed on her phone, and she leaves it running in the background. Phones produced after 2011 come equipped with GPS systems that are accurate to within twenty-five feet. Unless the Google Maps user has turned off the "allow Google to use location" option, Google receives location information from this phone as often as ten times a minute. With 80 percent of smartphones being Android devices that come shipped not only with Google Maps, but with the location option default set to "on," Google can easily determine whether traffic is flowing—or slowing. The bits transmitting users' phone locations stand in for direct observations of traffic once garnered by eye-in-the-sky traffic helicopters reporting on road congestion.[23]

We use bits to run experiments. Companies can use networks and sensors to see how devices work in the field. That's exactly what FANUC is doing with its networked robots; it is improving its customers' experience and learning how to improve the quality of its robots, all at the same time. The researchers at TigerPlace, the assisted living community in Missouri, are learning how sensors can best help the residents. How often should the sensors report on residents' movements? Too infrequently, and the nurses won't catch problems early enough. Too often, and batteries will need frequent changes, a quick way to convince residents and staff the system isn't worth it. Through testing, the researchers learned that every seven seconds was "just right." The ability to gather rapid feedback via networks allows researchers to test a system, modify it, and test again. Tweaking the system to improve performance takes a matter of hours or days, where once it might have taken months or years.[24]

We use bits to run systems at scale. Today's large, complex systems cannot plausibly be managed by hand. Consider the case of package delivery, a service Internet companies rely on to ship items to their customers. FedEx ships 1.25 billion packages a year, with its couriers traveling 900 million miles annually. The company has 300,000 employees and 43,000 delivery vans, yet somehow loses only 0.5 percent of the packages it ships. FedEx accomplishes this through an elaborate digital tracking system that lets the customer know where her package is every step of the way.[25]

Another example occurs with train switches. Even in today's networked, global economy, freight shipped by train occupies a surprisingly dominant place in global shipping. In the United States, for example, 40 percent of all freight is moved by train. For this older, yet still dominant, type of transportation infrastructure, the condition of the rails governs the overall efficiency of the system. Broken rails or welds cause 15 percent of rail accidents and 22 percent of freight-car derailments.[26]

The companies that manage train freight are aware of this situation. The traditional way to inspect the line involved sending people to look at the rails, a time-consuming—and person-consuming—process given the miles of tracks to inspect. But KONUX, a German company, is using sensors to digitize the inspection of Germany's railway tracks. The German rail company Deutsche Bahn controls 20,000 miles of railway track, with 70,000 switches. KONUX's technology dis-

tinguishes between normal vibration patterns and unusual
ones that indicate a potential problem. Even more striking, the
switch sensors on the railroad can identify *which* railway cars
are experiencing unusual vibrations and can flag those cars for
repair. Instead of having inspectors walk the train tracks, determining damage by staring at the rails, Deutsche Bahn manages maintenance at scale and from a distance, with networked
sensors.

Controlling action at a distance may in fact be the most
important change of all. As network connectivity became widely
available, workers began to expect remote control as a matter
of convenience. For managers, remote control reduced labor
costs, as one person sitting at a control panel could now do the
job of many. Sensors and actuators (devices for turning systems on and off) have brought the business of control at a distance to a whole new level.

When GE sells wind turbines—windmills for the twenty-
first century—it's not really selling huge, finely shaped pieces
of metal designed to catch the wind. Instead, it's creating wind
turbine owners to produce electrical power. Wind is variable;
it gusts, it flows, it shifts direction and shifts back. GE equips its
turbines with sensors to detect thirty different variables. The
sensors make readings several times a second that feed into
computers used to control the turbines. As wind conditions
shift, the computer fine-tunes various aspects of the blades to
respond accordingly. The result is greater energy production.[27]

Sitting here in my study, with its wooden bookshelves and
woolen rugs, I can almost convince myself that I'm in the same
world I was in when I set it up twenty-eight years ago. But the
arrival of networked computing has changed the way I do my

work. Two decades ago, when conducting research on US wire-tapping policy, I frequently visited the local university's government documents section to access reports. Now virtually all of these reports are online, including many whose existence predates the Internet. Twenty years ago, you needed a special conference number to talk to multiple people at once. Today my colleagues and I easily videoconference over Skype. My experience is not unique.

The increasing availability of fast networks drove the first stage of the Digital Revolution. We are on the cusp of the next stage, which is likely to increase the number of devices connected to the network a thousandfold. This will be a world in which switches not only report to Deutsche Bahn that car 218 417-4 is causing undue wear on the rails and needs to be inspected, but also do far more complex reporting—like using machine learning to determine from vibration data when switches are having problems. When my heart rate goes up, and I'm driving seventy miles an hour on the New Jersey Turnpike, listening to heavy metal, the sensors will merely take note. But if my heart rate goes up—and stays up—while I'm doing thirty miles an hour on a country lane, listening to Mozart, they'll report the data to my doctor.[28]

Networks make information from outside more accessible to those within an organization. Organizations can use this information to improve their internal decision making and actions. With networks, users on the inside can take advantage of services from outside, like cloud storage, to build their own capacity on the cheap. Networking also allows organizations to make better use of their own internal information, to improve efficiency and value.

These advantages come at a grave cost to security. Networks lower the effectiveness of borders. Determined hackers can now turn off the breakers at a switching station from thousands of miles away. They can increase the seriousness of their attacks. With the scale of networking vastly expanding, it's time we faced those risks.

3

Dangers Lurking Within

In August 1990, Iraq invaded its oil-rich neighbor Kuwait. Five months later, a United States–led coalition attacked Iraq and Kuwait. The first night of the 1991 war began with a process the Americans called "decapitating the enemy," in which coalition bombers launched weapons at Iraqi command and communications centers, destroying many of them. These successful attacks meant that from then on, the coalition forces largely owned the skies—and virtually everywhere else. Iraq was forced out of Kuwait after just five weeks of bombings, followed by a land war that lasted just 100 hours.[1]

Military leaders treasure military history because they need to understand what strategies and tactics work. It should be no surprise, then, that China's leaders paid close attention to the 1991 Gulf War. Chinese strategists saw how coalition forces won a battle against an entrenched enemy conducted thousands of miles from home. The Chinese leaders immediately grasped that the coalition's success depended on its ability to weave together command, control, communications, computers, intelligence, surveillance, and reconnaissance—C^{4}ISR, in military lingo.

At the time, China's military resembled Iraq's: heavy on personnel, light on advanced technology. If China wanted to win the wars of the future, it would need to replicate the coalition's ability to weave together people and technology. That meant a major transformation of China's military, weapons systems, communications, and surveillance capabilities.

US intelligence, watching from afar, tracked Chinese military developments with great interest. But US military strategists also knew that it would take time for China to carry out such a complex shift in its military structure. In 2004, the US Department of Defense acknowledged China's efforts to build a robust C⁴ISR system, but dismissed China's efforts as a threat. Instead, defense experts snobbishly reported that the People's Liberation Army's communication networks would "eventually" rival civilian networks elsewhere.[2]

In retrospect, this assessment underestimated the speed with which China's technical skills had evolved. By the mid-2000s, China was selling advanced switching technology to British Telecom, which was replacing its telephone network with one based on Internet packet switching. China was pressing ahead on cybersurveillance. In fact, by 2004, Chinese spies were already inside US communication networks. A 2005 *Time* magazine article reported that intruders had used unpatched vulnerabilities in NASA, World Bank, and US military computers to gain access. These were no accidental hacks. "They never hit a wrong key," said the analyst who discovered them in computer systems at Sandia National Labs. The attackers got in quietly, made targeted searches, then carefully packed up materials of interest. Among the materials they took were Army and Air Force helicopter and flight-planning software and detailed schematics for the Mars Orbiter. The bits disappeared into southern China.[3]

The US government response to all of this was muted. Perhaps the government didn't want to admit the extent of Chinese intrusions into Department of Defense networks, or perhaps the US government didn't actually know the extent of the intrusions. A more likely explanation, however, is that the United States didn't want to discuss cyberspying because US intelligence was actively conducting similar reconnaissance against other nations.

The private sector also started being targeted by Chinese hackers in the mid-2000s, though private-sector leaders, too, were slow to speak publicly about the threat. That changed in 2009, when Google became a target. The company learned that hackers had made off with some Google code for the company's password system. The hackers successfully accessed a database that included US surveillance targets (thus enabling the Chinese to determine which of their US agents had been compromised). They had also sought to breach the Gmail accounts of Chinese human rights activists. In some cases, the hackers did so successfully (including through placing malware—malicious software—on the activists' computers). When Google discovered the hacks, the company conducted an investigation and went public.[4]

During its investigation, Google uncovered evidence that many other companies had suffered similar intrusions and thefts. Hacker targets included computer software and hardware firms, defense contractors, chemical companies, and financial services. The hackers sought software, trade secrets, and business plans. Stolen data hopscotched its way to southern China, after which its path became untraceable. These thefts were no fly-by-night operations. The tools were not sophisticated, but the targets had been picked with care, and the attackers were persistent. They often used spear phishing, a personalized email that includes a link to an infected website with a request for information—but with a return email address that is not exactly what it appears be, or else an attachment in which malware lurks.[5]

Major defense contractors, including Lockheed Martin and Northrop Grumman, were among the targets. The Department of Defense believed that classified information regarding the development of a new fighter plane, the F-35, was secure, but wouldn't comment on the theft of unclassified information—and for good reason. Later, the Snowden disclosures revealed that multiple Department of Defense and defense contractor systems had been breached; 1,600 computers had been penetrated and 600,000 user accounts compromised. Stolen data included contractor research and development materials on the B-2, F-22, and F-35 jets, as well as on space-based lasers. Years later, when China unveiled its twin-engine J-31 fighter, the plane bore a striking resemblance to the F-35.[6]

China's cyberspying efforts extended across the globe. "Seventy percent of all major German companies are threatened or affected" by cyberattacks, a senior member of the German Ministry of the Interior reported. Chinese hackers sought to steal information from the European Aeronautic Defence and Space Company, which builds civilian and military aircraft and various other types of space and propulsion systems, as well as from ThyssenKrupp, a large producer of steel and equipment for heavy industry. The companies were just two of the numerous Asian and European businesses targeted by Chinese hackers. As in the United States, the hackers targeted advanced technologies in various economic sectors, including agriculture, electronics, pharmaceuticals, satellite communications, and solar power. Sometimes they stole diplomatic or military data, sometimes industrial information.[7]

Between 2006 and 2011, the security firm McAfee observed China-based cyberexploitation attacks against South Korean construction and steel companies; a Taiwanese electronics firm; a Singapore electronics company; several US defense contractors; US networking, communications, and information technology companies; Danish and US satellite communications companies; Taiwanese, Canadian, and US government agencies (both state and federal); a US national-security think tank; and a United Nations agency. The types of data stolen included computer code, email, business plans, contracts, and design schematics. The hackers took astonishing amounts of data, on the scale of petabytes. To give a sense of scale, the US Library of Congress collects a petabyte of data every four months (more romantically, if an average song lasts four minutes, then a petabyte of songs would provide 2,000 years of music). An NSA briefing showing five years of Chinese hacks revealed that only one state—North Dakota—had escaped attack. Whoever received this information discovered not only what the competition was doing now, but also what they planned for the future. This included business and pricing strategy as well as the development of new products.[8]

This was serious spying, apparently being conducted by a nation attempting to leapfrog its way to C⁴ISR and greater economic success. Nor was China the only nation worming its way into US networks and companies. Russia, Iran, and North Korea were also doing so. Apparently, so were some US allies.[9]

The United States, too, was using networks to spy. US spying differed from Chinese spying in a significant way: the United States did not share the information it learned with the private sector. In nations where the industries being surveilled by the United States were state-owned, this distinction seemed like splitting hairs. Through the 2000s, the number of intrusions and the attackers' capabilities steadily increased. But by the 2010s, attackers' interests were changing in disturbing ways, shifting to include not only cyberexploitation, but also cyberattack.

Let me briefly step back to explain this nomenclature. We talk about cyberattacks, but the 2009 incidents launched against Google and other US companies were cyberexploits. Cyberexploits steal data; cyberattacks destroy or disrupt a machine (or set of machines). Stealing engineering specifications for an F-35 is cyberexploitation, while the attacks on Sony's computers and the Ukrainian power grid, both described in Chapter 1, were cyberattacks. Cyberattacks take varied forms. As in the Sony case, a cyberattack might wipe computer hard drives. Or, as in the Ukrainian case, the attackers might change user passwords, thus preventing a legitimate user from exercising control and stopping the attack. An attacker might encrypt all of a victim's user files, offering to provide a decryption key in exchange for a ransom. Or attackers might use computer network connections to the physical world to launch physical attacks. The vast network of physical objects that is being connected to the network—the Internet of Things—has increased the dangers of this kind of destructive attack.[10]

Although cyberexploits and cyberattacks have different goals, they usually start with the same initial steps. Both need a way to get onto a victim's system. Malware might arrive via an email attachment (problematic if opened), a visit to an infected website, or a contaminated USB stick. The malware may be a worm, a self-replicating program that can spread within a computer or between computers; a virus, a self-replicating program fragment that must be part of a program to work; or a Trojan Horse, an attractive application that hides malicious behavior within it.

State-sponsored actors prefer Trojan Horses, which they operate through remote access; hence the term RAT, or Remote Access Trojan. A Trojan is typically installed through exploiting an unpatched vulnerability on the machine. Alternatively, a Trojan might enter through social engineering techniques. A piece of mail arrives, suggesting that the user download a certain app or visit a particular page, for instance. Once on the victim's computer, the malware begins conducting reconnaissance on her machine. It may be that the victim's machine is the target and the malware seeks information that's stored there. But the more likely situation is that the victim's machine is simply a way station to the actual target. The malware begins to gather several different pieces of information. What operating system and programs are running on the machine? What versions are they? Has the victim installed patches? The malware is looking for exploitable vulnerabilities, which are unintended flaws in the system that leave it open to attack. The attacker will also attempt to elevate the victim's privilege on the broader network, that is, seek to acquire access to resources to which the victim would not normally have rights.

As the attacker is searching the device, the attack software might use its beachhead to download additional malware. The ability to log into other systems is particularly valuable, so hackers sometimes install a key logger. This tool enables the attacker to capture a user's key strokes, thus learning the user's passwords to various accounts and other valuable information.

The attacker will want to learn about other potential devices on the network connected to this machine. Can these be directly accessed? Does the user need a credential, a digital security clearance, to access them? Are those credentials stored on this machine? Does the machine house other valuable files, such as credit card numbers, financial information, or proprietary business data?

The malware may send data back to the attackers while in the midst of the attack. Attackers may send information to the device. And in yet other cases, the attackers harness captured machines to carry out other attacks across networks. In denial-of-service attacks, for instance, hackers try to interrupt service by overloading the target with requests. In a distributed denial-of-service, or DDoS, attack, hackers use many compromised machines to strike at a single target, typically with the intent of bringing the target offline. When a single controller manipulates a set of infected machines, the group is called a botnet, and the individual hacked computers, which may appear to their user to be behaving normally, are known as bots, short for robot. Botnets may consist of hundreds of thousands—or even millions—of compromised computers.

In a case of cyberexploition, reconnaissance improves the quality of the information stolen. In a cyberattack, reconnaissance can improve the precision of an attack or possibly make it more destructive; it depends on the attackers' intentions. The Ukrainian power grid hackers, for example, studied the three distribution networks for six months before their attack. The preparation paid off. The three attacked systems went down within thirty minutes of each other. That's unlikely to be beginner's luck. The attackers had likely tested their attack software before they used it on the distribution centers, one of several indications that a powerful adversary—a nation—was behind this attack. By the time the hackers deployed their attack software on the Ukrainian systems, the attacks were devastatingly effective.

Cyberexploits and cyberattacks use many of the same tools. Cyberattacks need information, sometimes very precise information, about the system they are attacking. Thus until the final steps, when cyberexploits simply steal information whereas cyberattacks perform a destructive action, cyberexploits and cyberattacks look very similar. They break in, conduct reconnaissance, and send information out. This similarity may make it difficult for a network defender to know whether their system is "merely" being spied upon or is actually being prepared for an attack.

Throughout the 2000s, the US government tracked the Chinese cyberthreat but viewed other national security issues, including terrorism, as posing greater dangers. Cyberexploitation and cyberattacks did not even merit inclusion in the Department of Defense's annual worldwide national security threat assessment until 2008. But soon thereafter, concerns about the issue quickly climbed. The 2009 assessment described a "growing cyber threat" related to two distinct issues: DDoS attacks and financial theft by organized crime. The 2010 assessment went further, describing the cyberthreat as "far-reaching," with cyber listed first among the threats facing the United States. In 2011 and 2012, the declining fortunes of Al Qaeda and the question of its replacement, along with concerns about North Korea, took priority on the assessment. But from then on, cyber topped the list.[11]

That abrupt shift in threat priorities is somewhat mystifying. The first Internet-based attack occurred in 1986; the first attack that seriously disrupted the network happened two years later. As we have seen, cyberexploits have been a problem since early in the 2000s. So what changed in 2008? Understanding how and why cyberattacks took so long to be taken seriously requires a deeper foray into their thirty-year history.

The 1980s and early 1990s were the time of "let's see if we

can" attacks. The ARPANET, a project of the US Department of Defense, had been created in the late 1960s to enable computers in different locations to "talk" to each other and share resources. Its protocols had been developed to make it simple for computers to connect. In 1983, the administrators spun off a separate network for military facilities to share unclassified information, MILNET. By the mid-1980s, the civilian part of the ARPANET had become the Internet.

The first known cyberexploit came to light in 1986 because of a seventy-five–cent discrepancy in phone charges at Lawrence Berkeley Labs (LBL), a Department of Energy research laboratory in Berkeley, California. A seventy-five-cent anomaly in a cash register is just some missing coins, but such a discrepancy in a computer system is mysterious. Did it occur because of a programming error? Was it theft? What was happening?

LBL computer system administrator Cliff Stoll was asked to investigate. Stoll tracked the charge to an intruder whose account lacked a billing address. In the LBL systems, this was unusual; it meant the account hadn't been set up correctly. Stoll deleted the account, figuring that if the user complained, he could reinstate it properly. But then another user without an address turned up on the LBL systems. Stoll's concern grew.

Stoll began to track this intruder, observing him exploit a vulnerability and gain "superuser" status, which gave him the same type of privileges someone running the computer system would have. This would allow the intruder to get into other accounts. Following the intruder's activity on the LBL machines, Stoll watched him use a MILNET connection to log into the US Army Depot in Anniston, Alabama, which housed the Army's Redstone missile complex. Stoll could even see that the trespasser was attempting to obtain superuser privileges at the Army site, just as he had at LBL. But the intruder's ultimate intent remained unclear.[12]

Stoll sought help from the FBI. The Bureau scoffed at an investigation involving a loss of seventy-five cents; it didn't seem particularly bothered by the information-security issues. Stoll continued to investigate on his own, trying to enlist aid as he did so. With some effort, Stoll traced the intruder's connection as coming from nearby Oakland. Stoll enlisted the help of phone company technicians, and they traced the intruder's connection one step further back, to a defense contractor in McLean, Virginia. Unbeknownst to the contractor, the intruder was using the company's phone system to log into military installations around the United States.[13]

This intruder was relentless, making various attempts to gain greater access to systems he'd penetrated. He'd create accounts on different systems, leave them for a while, then return months later searching for material of interest: password files, military information, and so on. He was particularly interested in files that contained the expressions "SDI" (for Strategic Defense Initiative, a Reagan-era missile shield program), "nuclear," and "NORAD" (North American Aerospace Defense Command, which secures North American airspace). The intruder did his snooping with care, and he'd constantly check to see who else was on the system. He'd quickly log off if he detected a system manager online.

Stoll was just as relentless. Telephone technicians helped Stoll track the intruder to West German university systems in Bremen and Karlsruhe, to which he connected via dialup (as it was the 1980s and people connected to networks by dialing in from home). Stoll baited a "honey pot," creating computer files filled with fake memos and form letters about the SDI program. This lure kept the intruder on the LBL machine, making it easier to trace him. Stoll had also finally gotten the NSA's attention, and with it, the FBI's interest in the case. Ten months after Stoll first discovered the intruder, West German police arrested Markus Hess, who had been selling classified information to the KGB, the Soviet intelligence agency. Hess had downloaded files about sensitive US defense technologies from computers at US military installations and defense contractors. He was convicted of espionage.

The next major network attack, in 1988, brought the Internet to a standstill. A Cornell University graduate student, Robert Morris, Jr., wrote a self-replicating program that, once launched, reached out to "neighboring" computers and checked the new machines for certain well-known vulnerabilities. If any of these were present, Morris's program established an "authenticated" connection to the neighboring machine that allowed the originating device to infect the new machine with the tainted program. The newly infected computer then repeated the process.

The program's goal appears to have been to run undetected, and essentially harmlessly, on multiple machines. But Morris had allowed the worm to reinfect already affected systems one seventh of the time—too high a rate of reinfection—and infected machines slowly churned to a halt. System administrators quickly disconnected computers from the network, hoping to stave off infection and to prevent cleaned machines from getting reinfected. Systems were dropping off, and the network became a set of disconnected islands. In that sense, the "Morris Worm" served as the first denial-of-service attack on the Internet.[14]

The people who were trying to fix the problem couldn't connect over the network, complicating their ability to respond. They were accustomed to doing everything electronically, including looking up phone numbers. Now they couldn't even do that. Instead they were reduced to communicating via telephone or even fax—not very efficient means to fix computer code. One thing was clear: the Internet needed better mechanisms to respond to crises. DARPA, the US agency that had created the Internet's predecessor, the ARPANET, established a national Computer Emergency Response Team to be a security clearinghouse, sharing information about vulnerabilities and patches, that could additionally serve as an access point during a crisis.[15]

But Morris's program revealed a far more serious, and more fundamental, problem: the connections that powered the Internet made it vulnerable. The Internet was a communications network—it linked universities, research labs, and military facilities. But it was nothing like the other communications network that had been around for about a century: the telephone network. That network, or rather the telephone company that largely ran it, supplied phones, wires, a central office, and phone switches. The telephone company had a vested interest in keeping its network secure. The Internet, in contrast, is formed through the protocols that enable different sites to communicate with one another, but the underlying infrastructure belongs to many different players.

The Morris Worm didn't attack the network itself; it attacked the machines connected to the network. The responsibility for securing those computers fell to the individual sites. Each university, research lab, and military facility was in charge of securing its own system. And for many different reasons, they were failing to do so.

First, the Internet's precursor, the ARPANET, and then the Internet itself were developed as research, rather than "production," platforms. There was an underlying assumption that everyone on the network could be trusted. Designed to foster openness and sharing, rather than security, the network enabled users to share resources. This might be in the form of, for instance, access to supercomputers or sharing data. Thus many of the network-connected sites had accounts that permitted password-free access to anyone using the account name "guest." Attackers, including Stoll's intruder, took advantage of such easy access. Because system administrators were not expecting attackers, they and their users were somewhat casual in setting protections. In 5 percent of cases, the administrators hadn't bothered to change system defaults. If Stoll's intruder knocked on those doors, a default account name and password would let him in.[16]

Second, system administrators discounted both the skill level and the motivation of potential hackers. In the 1980s, system administrators believed their adversaries were teenagers and university students. They weren't expecting intrusions by proficient hackers and therefore did not develop protections to stop them.

The case of Stoll's intruder, Hess, is instructive. The hacker stole files of user passwords. These particular files did not contain the actual passwords, or even an encrypted form of the passwords. Instead, they contained a "hashed" version of the password. Hashes are a mathematical function that's easy to do in one direction, but difficult to reverse. They are encryption's equivalent of pouring a glass of water on the floor. When a user types a password, her machine creates a hashed version and compares it to the hashed version in the password file. The neat—and critical—feature of hash functions is that small changes in input are magnified in the hash. Thus, the hash of "wrong#" is "6d09a1cdc0dd6e4b5f2feddd9e73da5d1a ef2d8cd346aa0e23e656786bd140a3," but the hash of "wrang#"

is "b5ad8f591b395607c4a9bd91122b19097a4370d9039eccb095 f39bee2823cffc."[17]

With the password file in hand, Hess was in a position to try a "dictionary" attack. This consists of trying all possible passwords at leisure to see which ones match up to the hashed ones in the file. A casual hacker would not bother with such an effort, but a serious attacker would. The sites that Hess hacked had ways to protect against just this, for instance, by making the password files less accessible. But because the system administrators weren't anticipating sophisticated adversaries, they hadn't implemented these stronger protections.[18]

The third problem has less to do with the nature of the network, and more to do with the nature of humans. Depending on how it's configured, security can make using a computer much less convenient. For example, we're all told to use complex passwords, but a complex password on a home router complicates letting guests use the Internet. So, many people use simple passwords on their router, or even the default one (the more common defaults include "admin," "root," and "changeme" —not exactly hard to guess).

The Morris Worm took advantage of a simplification intended to make computers easier to use: "trusted hosts." This is just a list of computers that can access information from your computer without having to authenticate first. If my computer is on your computer's trusted hosts list, then my machine can use resources on yours without needing to present a password or other credential. That simplifies connections. Unfortunately, it makes them more easily compromised. On each computer it infected, the Morris Worm searched for that machine's trusted hosts; the worm was then able to propagate from one machine to another without having to log in to the next system. Removing trusted-hosts functionality prevents that aspect of the

Morris Worm attack—but it also makes sharing resources more complicated.

The flexibility that characterizes good computer code presents a fourth vulnerability. Good computer code is written to easily accommodate changes in functionality that weren't anticipated at the time the program was written. This flexibility comes at a cost, for it means that systems can be manipulated acting in ways their designers never intended. The Morris Worm provides an example of this.

The Morris Worm used sendmail, a program for handling Internet mail, to insert itself on other people's computers. Usually sendmail receives a mailbox address as input and delivers the mail there. But sendmail was designed so it could also deliver mail to a process. One such is a "vacation" program, which is invoked when sendmail delivers a piece of mail to the recipient. The vacation program is typically used to deliver an automatic response that the recipient is away and a reply will be delayed. Sendmail's ability to accept both addresses and commands as input is convenient; a user does not need to be a programmer to turn on the vacation response. The catch is that only message recipients should be able to turn on this feature of sendmail. But a small change in sendmail— in fact, a piece of code that was put in to simplify debugging that itself had an error in it—allowed senders to transmit a command. The debugging code's error on its own hadn't created a problem. But the Morris Worm combined the debugging code with the vacation program to transmit the worm *as a piece of computer code to be executed by the recipient's computer.*

Instead of mail, sendmail delivered an executable command that spread the Morris Worm. That brings up the fifth reason security was growing harder: as complex systems are combined, unexpected interactions can occur. And the chance for insecurity increases.

In the end, security is an out-of-pocket expenditure with no clear return. Implementing security has explicit costs in terms of both time and money, and enforcing security presents an entirely different set of costs. These costs may be perfectly legitimate but annoying. As a US government report noted, "Discussions of computer security frequently cite the trade-off between increased security and the sacrifices, in terms of convenience, system function, flexibility, and performance." In the 1980s, such trade-offs meant that security lost to convenience. And then it kept on losing.[19]

As we've seen, by the 1980s, the nascent Internet was connecting universities, research labs, the military, and others. In 1991 a British physicist working at a European particle acceleration laboratory in Geneva, Tim Berners-Lee, developed protocols that made it easy to post and fetch information from distant machines (these are the World Wide Web protocols, including the "http" you see when you download a webpage). Four years later, the Internet opened to commercial traffic and the boom began. As of this writing, fully half of humanity uses the Internet.[20]

E-commerce began shortly after the Internet went public, though no one was quite sure what "e-commerce" meant or how to do it in the 1990s. Should stores put only some of their wares online, using the Internet as an advertising medium to lure people into the shop? How should newspapers and magazines handle web publication? Should new stories go up as soon as they were written? Or should the online periodical simply act like an online version of the print edition, publishing a new edition once daily? These questions sound odd now.

But in the mid-1990s, no one understood how this medium would evolve.

Brick-and-mortar shops developed online presences, but many retailers saw them as additions to, not the core part of, their business plans. A few companies attempted a purely online existence, but no one really understood the business model. Indeed, Amazon.com, which now has the highest market capitalization of any US retailer, did not make a profit during its first five years. In part because the online sector remained so small, not much personal or corporate information was on the network in this early period.[21]

Except for webpage defacements, cyberexploits and cyberattacks in the 1990s largely targeted those with a greater presence on the network than online retailers. In 1998, after hackers broke into government systems—including the Department of Defense and the Department of Energy (where nuclear weapons research is conducted)—the United States started taking such threats much more seriously. Hackers' forays into these systems, as well as those of universities and research centers, yielded thousands of files with unclassified information on military plans and scientific work. Hacking had become a problem too serious to ignore.[22]

In 1999 and 2000, two broad-based attacks highlighted the risks of the newly popular, easy-to-use email programs. The Melissa and ILOVEYOU viruses traveled in email attachments that accessed Microsoft users' address books. The virus then copied itself and sent a copy to addresses in the contact list. The process started as soon as a recipient opened the attachment. Melissa emailed itself to the first fifty names on a user's address list; ILOVEYOU, to everyone on the list. Melissa was said to have spread to 100,000 computers, ILOVEYOU to many times that. The result was clogged systems and, in ILOVEYOU's case, overwritten music and photo files (an additional present from its writer).[23]

The next year (2001) saw an attack with far more serious consequences. In mid-June Microsoft announced a patch for a coding error found on its IIS webservers. Three weeks later, a relatively innocuous worm attacking unpatched systems was released; it caused little damage. The programmers who dealt with the problem named it CodeRed, in honor of the caffeinated soft drink they consumed to stay awake while they analyzed the worm. A variant, released a week later, was much worse. Named CodeRedII, it infected over 350,000 computers in less than fourteen hours. Once on a computer, CodeRedII created a back door so the worm could receive communication from a controller. Twenty-four hours later, the worm would go to work, rebooting the computer and then simultaneously probing hundreds of other computers. The worm first sought to infect other systems; then it launched a DDoS attack against a predetermined site. Then the worm rested.[24]

In combining two forms of malware—a worm for spreading and a DDoS attack—CodeRedII presented a double whammy. The worm's spread clogged the Internet and then created chaos in its wake. The initial DDoS target was www1.whitehouse .gov; the attack forced the White House to move its Internet address to remain publicly accessible. The attacks affected other organizations as well. The US Department of Defense briefly shut down some public websites; the Department of the Treasury's Financial Management Service went offline; Qwest, a large telecommunications carrier in the western United States, experienced nationwide outages in its ISP service; and FedEx failed to meet its delivery promises. All this took place in 2001, when the Digital Revolution's penetration of everyday commerce was only a fraction of what it is today.[25]

Microsoft was in trouble. In prioritizing being first to market and making its products usable, the company had never emphasized security. Coding is complex, both because programs must allow for many different path-dependent scenarios, and because programs are combined in unexpected ways, sometimes long after they are written. People make mistakes when they code. Small programs, of one hundred lines or so, may be free of errors, but large ones cannot be. Something like the Windows 10 operating system has on the order of 50 million lines of code. Nevertheless, over the last half-century, software engineers have learned some best practices. The security vulnerability that enabled the CodeRed attacks exploited a buffer overflow, a programming flaw known since 1972. That never should have happened. The connections of the Internet had raised the stakes of programming errors. Microsoft could no longer afford lax security for its products.

"By the end of 2001, no Microsoft executive could have any conversation with any enterprise customer about anything but Microsoft's bad security," said Steve Lipner, who was the company's director of security assurance at the time. Microsoft began to make security a priority. In early 2002, all 8,500 Windows developers underwent security training. They then spent February and March reviewing code for security flaws, finding bugs and fixing them, fixing default settings to be on secure mode, and so on. Microsoft began embedding security into its product development process, and that has made a serious difference. Indeed, Microsoft's Security Development Lifecycle, a process for integrating security into product development, has now been adopted by Cisco and Adobe.[26]

Early Internet attacks had consisted of the stealthy theft of military secrets and a cowboylike grandstanding by hackers showing off their ability to attack systems. In the early 2000s, as people and companies moved more and more data onto Internet-accessible systems, the nature of attacks expanded. The problem of stealing information, whether for criminal purposes or for economic espionage, became serious.

The Digital Revolution enabled certain new crimes, though fewer than people imagine. Denial-of-service attacks became an effective method of disruption—and extortion—as businesses and governments moved the site of their contact with the public from shopfronts and phones to online. Identity theft, the misuse of an individual's identity information, became simpler to accomplish, given the amount of personal information available online. That said, the vast majority of identity theft cases simply involve stealing a credential, such as a credit card number, rather than manufacturing a full new identity based on stolen information.[27]

Online credential stealing appears to have begun in the late 1990s when AOL, the leading provider of Internet access, required a credit card number to open an account. Criminals pretending to be account managers would send email to AOL users asking them to confirm their billing information. Sometimes users were asked to click on links that sent them to spoofed sites (paypa1.com rather than paypal.com) that collected the information. Over time, hackers developed methods to steal credentials on a much larger scale, usually by stealing them directly from companies. By 2005, criminals were accessing poorly protected corporate systems and collecting millions of pieces of credit card information, including accountholder names, credit card numbers, and expiration dates.

Credit card thieves developed various ways to find their way into these corporate systems. One was through "war driving," in which a criminal uses unencrypted store WiFi networks to access the companies' main servers. Others placed packet sniffers, a tool for intercepting data, in company networks to collect credit card data, which was then used to make counterfeit cards. The thefts were aimed at such household names as Barnes and Noble, Target, and TJX (owners of TJ Maxx and Marshalls), subjecting the general public to the ills arising from hacking. Similar hacking techniques were used to place a packet sniffer within Heartland Payment Systems, a payment-processing provider that handles about 100 million transactions monthly. The illegal tap collected unencrypted card information as the data traveled between servers at the processing company.[28]

The Internet also simplified the crime of bank robbery. Instead of threatening tellers with guns or tunneling and blasting into a bank vault, hackers found their way into the systems of RBS WorldPay, the US processing arm of the Royal Bank of Scotland. The hackers created forty-four counterfeit debit cards with notably higher cash limits than the normal ones. All that remained was to convert the cards into cash. Working in just twelve hours, a network of "mules" did exactly that. They withdrew money from 2,100 ATM sites across Canada, Estonia, Hong Kong, Italy, Japan, Russia, Ukraine, and the United States. The heist netted $9 million—until the criminals were caught.[29]

While the scale of Internet-based financial crimes is growing, their financial cost is unclear. The US Department of Justice documents losses in these cases amounting to hundreds of millions of dollars, but hard evidence concerning the full scale of the problem is absent. Many researchers have noted that the numbers don't look right. For example, the Federal Trade Commission estimated the cost of identity theft as $47 billion in 2006, $15.6 billion in 2007, $54 billion in 2008. Such wide swings indicate that—for reasons that remain unclear—

somehow the sampling wasn't done sufficiently carefully. A more reliable number comes from the US Federal Reserve, which arrived at a number of $3.7 billion for credit and debit card losses due to fraud in 2006. But whatever the correct numbers are, it is clear that, by the late 2000s, efforts to steal credit card numbers were growing in sophistication and scale and making the criminals a lot more money—even if no one was sure exactly how much.[30]

Having to deal with a stolen credit card number is unpleasant for the victim, but there's a streamlined process in place to fix it. But the process of tracking down and prosecuting perpetrators is complicated. It's not easy to pin online theft to any particular set of users. Intruders attempt to hide where they're coming from. This is relatively easy to do in the networked world: think back to Stoll's intruder, who hopped, skipped, and jumped through other computer systems until he reached his target. Once the criminals have what they want, they hop, skip, and jump backwards and effectively disappear.

If the cyberthief reaches into your system from a system to which you have a connection—a system administrator you can contact, an ISP willing to trace the path of information in and out of the other system—then you can begin to trace the theft backwards. That's what Stoll did in tracing his wily hacker. In that sense, Stoll was lucky. His hacker used systems that were only in "friendly" territory, that is, countries with a good record of legal cooperation. Once Stoll had proper legal authorization —and that took time to obtain—West German telecommunications providers put traces on the hacker's calls to the university computer systems to find out the number he was dialing from.

Such situations are the exception rather than the rule in cyberincidents. If an attacker or stolen files are traced to Russia, China, or certain other locations, legal cooperation typically stops at that point. Without legal cooperation, an investigator's ability to use tracking technology to figure out if the last place the data was seen was indeed the intended destination or just a way station, essentially ends. That's why the attribution problem—determining who is stealing and who is attacking—can be very difficult to solve.

But the Digital Revolution not only creates the possibility for new types of crimes; it also offers new tools for criminal investigation. Even with limited international cooperation, the wired society provides a much richer evidentiary environment than law enforcement has ever had, markedly changing the opportunities for investigation.

By the late 2000s, cyberattacks began to target nation-states. Much of this was hidden, but a 2007 DDoS attack on Estonia brought the phenomenon to public light. This small nation on the Baltic has a million and a half people, 70 percent of whom identify as Estonian and 25 percent as ethnic Russians (most of the latter having come during the time that Estonia was part of the Soviet Union).

After World War II, when the USSR defeated German forces in Eastern Europe, the Russians stayed. The Soviet Union absorbed the countries of Estonia, Lithuania, and Latvia. There the three Balkan nations remained until the fall of the USSR in 1991. At that point Estonia turned west, joining NATO in 2004. Some remnants of the Soviet annexation endured, however. One was a six-foot-high bronze statue of a Soviet soldier. In April 2007, the Estonian government moved this memorial from downtown Tallinn, the Estonian capital, to a cemetery several kilometers away. The ethnic Russian population protested, and rioting began in the capital. When the rioting ended, the nation came under electronic attack.

Russian websites urged Russian patriots to conduct DDoS attacks on Estonia, providing instructions on how to do so. Estonia was, at this point, a highly wired nation; it viewed itself, with some reason, as "E-stonia." Already in 2005 the nation had conducted a national election via the Internet; 60 percent of the country's population used the Internet daily.[31]

Hackers attacked Estonian websites, newspapers, banks, and the government for almost a month. They launched at least 128 separate attacks in the first two weeks, largely against government sites: the Estonian police, Ministry of Finance, Parliament, and the prime minister's office. Estonian sites suffered DDoS attacks, and some websites were defaced. As the nation coped, Estonian network engineers saw that the attack originated outside the country. In the first several days, Estonia electronically severed international connections to the Internet whenever an attack began. Soon the engineers identified less disruptive solutions that cut off the hackers while still allowing the rest of the world in. The attack ended of the hackers' own accord after three weeks.[32]

Who did it? NATO concluded it was not the Russian government, although clearly individual Russians egged this effort on. In some sense, the most important lesson of the attack was that cyberattacks could target a nation-state's ability to function.[33]

A year later, another nation at odds with Russia, Georgia, suffered a DDoS attack. South Ossetia, a region that lay between the two nations, had been a point of conflict between the two countries since 1991, when the region essentially separated from Georgia during the fall of the Soviet Union. In late July 2008, Georgia began experiencing cyberattacks: webpage defacements, DDoS attacks against government websites, and efforts to distribute malicious software to members of the Georgian government. In August 2008, Georgia began a military campaign against separatist action in South Ossetia. Within a day, Russian troops and armored vehicles entered the breakaway region while bombers hit targets in Georgia itself. A military ceasefire between Russia and Georgia was arranged within days, but the cyberattacks against Georgian systems continued for a number of weeks.[34]

In contrast to the situation in Estonia, Georgia had only a weak Internet presence. The attack primarily affected the government's web presence, rather than the private sector's, because so little of the Georgian private sector relied on online services. During the conflict, the Georgian government censored the Internet, but because the Russians had damaged Georgian broadcast transmitters, the government was effectively silenced during the height of the attacks. The combination meant that little news was available to the public, which created some panic among the Georgians that the Russians were invading their country.[35]

The attacks were apparently conducted by private citizens coming to the patriotic aid of the Russian government when it was in conflict with Georgia—although how disconnected these citizens actually were from the Russian government is unclear. The botnets were launched through systems controlled by the Russian Business Network, a Russian criminal organization that, if not connected to the government, is certainly tolerated by it. This was the first, but hardly the last, indication of the way that Russia might use cyberattacks against other nations.[36]

Eventually, it was inevitable that cyberattacks on nation-states would make the jump from disruption and vandalism to attacking critical infrastructure and military installations. Although the perpetrators hoped to keep the matter quiet, the public finally learned of one such attack in 2010. I am speaking here of Stuxnet, the US-Israeli cyberweapon targeted against Iran's nuclear facility in Natanz.

Iran signed the Treaty on the Nonproliferation of Nuclear Weapons in 1968. This treaty obliges nonnuclear nations to forgo building nuclear weapons in exchange for aid for civilian nuclear energy. In 2002, US intelligence satellite photos provided evidence that Iran was building a heavily fortified, underground nuclear weapons facility in Natanz. Several years earlier the International Atomic Energy Agency, which monitors treaty compliance, had learned that Iran was attempting to purchase centrifuge parts. Centrifuges are critical; they separate the isotope of uranium needed for weapons, U_{235}, from its more common variant, U_{238}. The agency began to monitor Natanz.

By 2006, Iran's ability to enrich uranium had improved dramatically. Israel, which does have nuclear weapons, expressed great concern to the United States about Iran's progress. Because of Israel's earlier actions against nearby nations' nuclear capabilities—in 1981 Israeli bombers had destroyed an Iraqi nuclear reactor—the US took Israeli concerns about the Iranian nuclear effort seriously. In 2009, odd things began to happen to the Iranian centrifuges. An uninterruptible power source that Iran had bought from Turkey began having power surges, destroying the Iranian centrifuges. A bit later, more subtle problems began to emerge. The centrifuges began breaking at a surprising rate, and Iranian scientists struggled to identify the cause of the problem. It turned out that the centrifuges were being run at speeds far higher than that those for which they'd been designed, but this information did not show up on the control panels.[37]

The network running the centrifuges had been attacked by Stuxnet, a computer worm. Stuxnet was designed to unleash its malware only if the network device controlling the centrifuges was of a type used at Natanz—these were relatively uncommon—and only if the centrifuge configuration was the same at Natanz. This was, in other words, a Natanz-specific worm.[38]

Most cyberattacks target low-hanging fruit, introducing malware through the use of a known, but unpatched, vulnerability. Stuxnet used "zero days," vulnerabilities that are unknown to, and unpatched by, the software maker. The term arose from there being no time—zero days—from the moment a vulnerability was known until it could be used. Now cybersecurity experts use the term "zero day" more generally to refer to any vulnerability unknown by the manufacturer at the time the vulnerability is used.

Zero-day vulnerabilities are most prized when they work against widely deployed systems—and Stuxnet's were all located in the Windows operating system, which made them particularly valuable. Stuxnet's designers had identified not just one zero day, but five, an extraordinary number. Each served a different purpose. Two of the vulnerabilities escalated privileges, one enabled the worm to spread inside the network, and one inserted malware onto the centrifuge controllers. The fifth also would have escalated privileges, but was patched by Microsoft along the way, and so fell out of the plans. Stuxnet had other tricks as well. Manufacturers use digital certificates to authenticate code as legitimate. Stuxnet used either stolen keys or stolen credentials to sign the malware, making it appear that it was from trusted providers. This fooled the Natanz systems into trusting the malware.[39]

The expense and sophistication of Stuxnet left no doubt

about the seriousness of the attack. To prevent its discovery, the worm recorded the centrifuge network controllers' normal behavior and played it back even as the malware ran the centrifuges at abnormally high speeds. Anyone looking at the control panel would see data indicating normal operations. This trick enabled the destruction to go on for quite some time.

The worm eventually escaped the Natanz facility through a mistake in its programming. As had been intended, Stuxnet caused no damage outside of the Iranian nuclear facility, but the makers of antivirus software started analyzing it. They found Stuxnet to be the most complex worm they had ever seen. As they deconstructed it, they began publishing their findings in blog posts. Stuxnet's precise targeting allowed the antivirus makers to identify Natanz as the object. Shortly thereafter, workers at Natanz shut down the centrifuges and presumably scrubbed the network of the worm.[40]

Over time the news came out that Stuxnet had been a joint effort of the United States and Israel. Not unexpectedly, Iran retaliated—but not against Israel. Instead, Iran targeted Saudi Arabia, a US ally. In August 2012, a computer virus attacked Saudi Aramco, destroying data on three-quarters of the computers on the company's business network and wiping clean the boot drives, destroying the machines. (The virus did not reach the network that controlled oil production.) A month later, a number of major US banks were subject to massive DDoS attacks. This attack, too, was attributed to Iran.[41]

With Stuxnet, cyberattacks had entered a new era. The United States and Israel had crossed a line by deploying the world's first known offensive cyberweapon. But it is also the case that what Stuxnet accomplished—a delay in Iran's development of a nuclear weapon without loss of life—was almost universally agreed to be a good thing. The attack, however, underscored the lack of clear rules for the use of cyberweapons.

Over the centuries, nations have developed well-understood norms for responding to physical attacks from other nations. For instance, when a Chinese pilot forced a US Navy plane conducting surveillance over the South China Sea to land in 2001, the United States did not threaten to go to war over the issue despite the breach in behavior. (The US plane and crew were returned, but not before the Chinese government had a chance to study much of the secret data.) But in cyber the rules are unclear. Might a cyberattack trigger a physical response rather than a cyberattack in kind? And what would "in kind" mean? In part because the potential consequences vary so much, countries have struggled to reach consensus on this issue. Wired nations are at much greater risk, and want very different rules than those whose systems are much less at risk. The presence of private actors, both as victims (such as Sony and the Las Vegas Sands Corporation, which suffered an Iranian attack of a similar nature) and as aggressors (such as private Russian citizens attacking Estonian sites), complicates the situation.[42]

Until recently, hackers assumed that they would be able to successfully hide their origins by routing their attacks through other people's machines. But such disguises go only so far and work less well today than they once did. In 2013 the cybersecurity firm Mandiant used publicly available data, including Google searches and Facebook posts, to expose three Chinese hackers from the People's Liberation Army unit most responsible for cyberexploits against US and Western industry. The US government was even willing to indict five Chinese hackers by name (one of them, "Ugly Gorilla," was also named in the Mandiant report). But having indicted the hackers, the United States has not attempted to remove them from China. From the intelligence community's perspective, that's just as well, because not holding a trial removes the need to disclose the methods by which it learned the hackers' true identities.[43]

The Snowden disclosures in 2013 revealed the remarkable extent of the NSA's intelligence collecting around the world. The NSA's spying included but was not limited to collecting data traveling between Google and Yahoo data centers (that is, collecting information of Google and Yahoo users); wiretapping Angela Merkel, François Hollande, and other leaders of nations friendly to the United States; eavesdropping on various companies; and collecting, in bulk, domestic communications metadata. US citizens, allies, and adversaries alike reacted with fury over the scale of collection. Merkel, normally a great friend of the United States, was livid, comparing the eavesdropping to that of the Stasi, the secret police in the former East Germany. The Snowden disclosures also revealed that the United States had spied on foreign companies. Brazil, whose oil and gas company Petrobras was among the targets, discussed requiring that data of Brazilians be stored within the country, a change that would disrupt businesses such as Google and Facebook.[44]

The nature of cyberattacks makes it difficult to discern an attacker's intent. It's not always easy to tell if a gunshot from across a border was fired by someone accidentally shooting a BB gun while hunting squirrels, by someone testing your reaction, or by someone actively trying to shoot you. In the summer of 2013, for instance, an Iranian hacker accessed the control systems of a dam in Rye, New York. This was not a random action; the hacker was one of the group that had helped launch the DDoS attacks against US banks. In theory, the hacker's access to the dam's controls might have allowed a small flood; in practice, nothing happened. The dam controls were offline due to maintenance, and the dam itself was small. Was this intrusion simply meant as a signal that Iran could attack critical infrastructure in the United States? Or had the attacker mistaken the dam for a much larger one in Oregon that happened to have a similar name?[45]

Cyberattacks have been increasingly common weapons in political battles. The South China Sea is an area of territorial conflict, but it has also become an area of cyberconflict between China and two of its opponents, Vietnam and the Philippines. In 2014, Vietnam gained the dubious honor of most targeted nation for cyberattacks. The reason? China appeared to be collecting intelligence on Vietnamese government websites to support a Chinese company that had placed an oil rig in Vietnamese territorial waters. Two years later, Chinese hackers targeted the Philippines when the Permanent Court of Arbitration in The Hague rejected China's claims in the South China Sea in a case brought by the Philippines. Filipino government sites were taken offline for days.[46]

In 2014 and 2015, Chinese hackers scored a major victory against the United States, penetrating the US Office of Personnel Management (OPM) and taking the files of 21 million people—not just *all* federal employees, but also those who had applied for US government security clearances. This included information not just about the person seeking clearance, but about her friends and family. The files included financial data, psychological records, information on drug and alcohol use, and in some cases fingerprints. The OPM collects such information to assess whether a candidate for clearance might be subject to blackmail; now it was in the hands of people who might do exactly that. The data thieves were also in a position to identify US spies posted abroad.

The hackers accomplished this intelligence feat in the standard way: a stolen credential enabled them to enter the government system in 2014. The credential apparently came from a contractor, but was nevertheless sufficient to get the hackers into the OPM's networks. Because the government agency had not required multifactor authentication, that was all it took. After that, the hackers conducted extensive reconnaissance and installed a tool that simplified and helped hide their work as they downloaded extraordinarily large numbers of files.[47]

Another group—or possibly the same group?—of Chinese hackers used similar techniques to steal the health records of 80 million people from the US health insurer Anthem/Blue Cross in 2015. Health records are not credit card data, so there was no immediate impact. But the wealth of information such records contain means that they can be used in multiple ways: for blackmail, for tracking users, and for identity theft. The information disclosed in health records grants thieves enough information to establish false identities that can then be used to create or take over accounts.

Why would criminals go to such an effort? With chip-and-PIN credit cards, the financial companies have made counterfeiting cards more difficult. In response, criminals are moving to online fraud, which means they need other kinds of authentication credentials. Criminals use automated methods to simplify the process of guessing authentication credentials. Suppose, as is commonly the case, that the card uses the expiration date for authentication. A criminal may take one account number and, at forty-eight different sites, try that number with all possible combinations of months and years for the next four years (12/17, 01/18, 02/18, and so on). One of those will work; that's the correct expiration date for that card number.

But with identity theft, criminals can use stolen personal information to take over accounts or create new ones. Point-of-sale credit card fraud is now down; losses due to fraudulent applications, lost or stolen cards, and account takeover are increasing. Both account takeover and the creation of fraudulent accounts rely on stolen identity information. Or, as one Silicon Valley security firm has noted, "Identity has now truly become a 'currency' with many fraudsters focused on augmenting existing identity credentials." If the bad guys know enough about you, they can create accounts in your name, commit an online theft, collect the funds, and disappear long before you get home from work.[48]

Several years ago, some in the US military predicted a "cyber Pearl Harbor," perhaps in the form of a crippling cyberattack on national infrastructure. Although cyberattacks do occur and have accompanied military efforts, many analysts have now abandoned that mode of thinking. Instead of attacks, we are now confronted with something that might best be described as cybermischief. Such efforts can be every bit as devastating as genuine attacks.

Consider Russia's theft of emails from the Democratic National Committee and other political organizations during the 2016 presidential campaign and the subsequent publication of this mail by WikiLeaks. The publication of the Clinton team's sharp assessments and political calculations created a steady drip, drip, drip of negative news in the months and weeks leading up to the November election. As the director of national intelligence said, "These thefts and disclosures [were] intended to interfere with the US election process."[49]

It is impossible to know what caused the surprise victory of Donald Trump. Trump's margin of victory in the three states that won him the Electoral College was a total of 77,000 votes, a number small enough to have easily been influenced by the months of leaks. If indeed the Russian cyberexploit and consequent publication had this effect, Russia's actions demonstrate how easily cybermischief, no matter how many steps removed from acts of war, may accomplish quite devastating attacks on one's adversaries.

Russia is employing similar tactics elsewhere. The same Russian group that hacked the DNC also stole mail from French candidate Emmanuel Macron ahead of that nation's presidential elections in 2017. At the time of this writing, Russia is believed to be directing similar efforts against German politicians. There are hints of similar attempts in Norway and the Netherlands as well.[50]

The Russian attack is different in kind from the types of attacks—Stuxnet, Saudi Aramco, Sony—that policymakers and military leaders had anticipated. Military and government systems remain potential targets of attack, and industry is still in the crosshairs of those who would like to steal its secrets. But the Russian cyberexploit against US political parties—and against parties in other nations—demonstrates a threat to civil society that is more difficult to combat.

Next time will Russia's target be an American blogger posting on US policy on Ukraine? An American businessman crossing Russian oil interests? A French journalist publishing on Russian intrigue in the French election? The recent Russian cyberexploit exposes the soft underbelly of wired societies, particularly wired societies that prize some level of open exchange. How can large swathes of society secure themselves against a determined nation-state that wants to steal their secrets?

4

How Do We Protect Ourselves?

Ignoring cyberthreats won't make them go away. Nor is it possible to build some sort of virtual wall to keep the bad guys off the Internet. As CIA director George Tenet pointed out in 1998, "We share the same network with our adversaries." How, then, can we protect ourselves from the growing risks of cyberexploits and cyberattacks?[1]

Case-by-case responses to cybersecurity crises may be tactically appropriate, but they rarely get at the underlying problem. In 2014, in considering how US national security should handle cyberinsecurity, former Secretary of the Navy Richard Danzig focused on the essentials. He drew the obvious, yet important, conclusion that the first step should be to determine what, from a national security perspective, needed to be protected. Once the assets had been prioritized, those systems should be made as simple as possible. "Strip down," Danzig wrote. "Strip systems so that they do less but have fewer vulnerabilities."[2]

Danzig's recommendations were based on the idea that a computer system pared down to essentials is easier to secure. That's because sometimes features interact in unexpected ways, creating vulnerabilities. Simple systems are easier to secure, yet can still carry out impressive tasks. For instance, DARPA, the agency that brought the world the Internet, developed an essentially unhackable helicopter—the key word here being "essentially." Pieces of the helicopter software were verified to be correct, meaning that they had no bugs that made them vulnerable to usual hackers (but not necessarily secure against, say, hackers with ray guns that can change bits in the code).[3]

As part of the verification process, DARPA assigned a team of skilled, well-funded hackers the job of breaking into the system. Even with more time and resources than actual hackers would have had, they couldn't make a dent in the security. Even though these tests could not rule out the potential damage caused by a team of dedicated, state-sponsored hackers, the ability to withstand assault from a highly skilled, well-supplied group of hackers was impressive.[4]

Though a significant achievement, DARPA's ability to create a relatively secure helicopter depended on tightly circumscribed circumstances. Two key pieces of the code were deemed unhackable: the software controlling communications between the helicopter and the ground; and a small, but critical, piece of the operating system. Securing the communications software is crucial: prevent the enemy from accessing the communications code and you've prevented him from changing instructions to the machine. And the secure critical piece of the operating system prevents untrusted code from making changes to systems controlling the helicopter's basic functionality such as lift, direction, and so on. Such constraints—where security trumps functionality and efficiency—are typical in military settings, but rarely apply in the context of industry or civil society. This particular case suggests the potential of securing the trusted piece in the operating system, in that it means that unsecured applications could be used if they had a limited role.

Try reproducing the secure helicopter experience for a consumer item—say, a car or a smartphone—and you immediately run into trouble. Cars, for instance, have multiple communication channels. Drivers and their passengers insist on having access to entertainment systems, Bluetooth, and GPS. Connected cars—arriving soon—will have vehicle-to-vehicle and cloud communication. Smartphones rely on apps, which, while vetted to various degrees by an app store provider, are essentially uncontrolled. Both cars and smartphones are large, complicated systems with lots of frequently changing parts. But the essentially unhackable helicopter does have a good security story for the rest of us. It is possible to write simple pieces of code for simple systems—think devices for the Internet of Things—that are relatively unhackable. And that's very good news indeed.

In a rush toward efficiency, the builders of the Digital Revolution brought together complex systems without necessarily considering the consequences. Marty Edwards, who directs the Industrial Control Systems Cyber Emergency Response Team at the Department of Homeland Security, talked to me about this problem in the context of manufacturing plants and the power grid. "In some cases," he told me, "we've overcomplicated them. We expect them to run to extremes, want to push these systems to optimum. Not just the grid, but also manufacturing." He paused, and then added, "We've allowed policies of efficiency to drive us into [a situation] where there is too much cyber risk." Pulling these systems off a network would reduce risk, but with production costing more and yielding less, managers are unlikely to adopt this approach.[5]

Meanwhile, on the factory floor, "There's no authentica-

tion, period." Ralph Langner—the person who told me this—
is an expert in the control systems used in power plants and
factories and played a key role in analyzing Stuxnet. In factories, a person's physical presence acts as a form of authentication (a newcomer on the factory floor stands out). Computer
authentication schemes are weak. "Shared passwords are the
norm," Langner said, "and in most cases, people never log off."
Many people connect to the factory floor. "The average factory
today relies on ten to 500 contractors, outside service providers," said Langner. "They connect via remote access, or physically onsite with their own laptop." Networking exposes factories and critical infrastructure to new threats, but owners only
rarely understand this. Their response is typically, "Why would
anyone cyberattack us?"[6]

In recent years, many of the larger companies have become aware of such threats and protected themselves accordingly. But industry in the United States is decentralized, with
over 300,000 companies having fewer than 500 employees. For
the most part, smaller companies do not understand the dangers of these threats. Their insecurity endangers others as well
as themselves. As with contractors, hackers can use the low
defenses of small companies to worm their ways into larger,
well-protected ones, making the larger company vulnerable
after all through its relationships with small companies.

Security experts have recommended a variety of solutions, only some of which are being implemented. Patching,
for instance. Monitoring the network to find anomalous behavior and stopping it. The adoption of stripped-down systems,
where possible. And then there's data encryption, and especially preventing attackers from getting credentials in the first
place. The chief of the NSA's Tailored Access Operations organization, Rob Joyce, notes that login credentials are the most

valuable data for attackers. Once hackers have that—however briefly—they have a beachhead on your system. All this brings us to the Crypto Wars.[7]

The current conflict over encryption has been forty years in the making. When the fight first began in the 1970s, the National Security Agency clashed with the private sector over whether certain sensitive areas of cryptographic research could be published. Later, the NSA and the private sector butted heads over whether the NSA would control the development of cryptographic standards for civilian agencies. NSA lost both battles.[8]

In the 1990s, with Internet commerce starting, the fight over cryptography once again heated up. Customers wanted computer systems with secure communications; otherwise how could you do business? But the last thing the NSA wanted was to make encryption easier for everyone across the world; how would it listen in abroad? Controls of equipment with military uses—fighter planes, tanks—started during the Cold War. The controls extended to so-called dual-use technologies with both military and civilian applications. Thus, if a computer or communications system had encryption capabilities, it needed an export license to be shipped abroad—a slow process. In the 1990s, the US government gave manufacturers a way out: easy export for devices with very weak encryption systems. But the Internet was booming, and this "solution" wasn't working for the companies. The resulting debate over appropriate limits to encryption came to be known as the First Crypto War.[9]

That battle ended in 2000, with a loosening in export controls that largely satisfied industry. Sales to governments and communications services, and sales of custom-built systems, were still tightly regulated, but essentially all other sales could skip the export license process. But then a new war over encryption emerged, not just over communications, but also over secured devices. We're in the midst of the Second Crypto War now.

Making sense of the two Crypto Wars—the first over export controls, the second that came to a head over the locked terrorist iPhone discussed in Chapter 1—requires a brief dip into encryption terminology. A cryptosystem consists of an algorithm, which is simply a method for encrypting, and a secret piece of information, the key, that is used in conjunction with the algorithm. Both concepts are best explained by example.

In the example that follows, I use a small letter to denote the unencrypted form and a capital letter for its encrypted version. In the Caesar shift, a two-thousand-year-old algorithm used by the Roman leader, each letter of the alphabet is shifted some number of letters; for instance, an "a" might be encoded by a "D," a "b" by an "E," a "z" by a "C," and so on (in this case, the encrypted version of "cab" would be "FDE"). The shift is the algorithm; the amount of the shift (three letters in this case) is the key. A slightly more interesting encryption system would mix the letters randomly; an "a" might be encoded by a "D," a "b" by a "Q," a "c" by an "M," and so on, with the encoding chosen at random (but ensuring that no letter is used twice). This algorithm is a "substitution cipher"; the key would be the twenty-six-letter table that lays out the substitution. (Because of the frequency in which certain letters, pairs of letters, triples, and so on appear in a language, a trained cryptanalyst can decrypt a message encoded with a substitution cipher with only a small portion of encrypted text.) Key length is the number, in bits, of the length of the key, and it's one aspect of how secure an encryption algorithm is.[10]

Since the key in the Caesar cipher is an integer between 0 and 25, the cipher's key length is 5. That's because the largest key is 25, written in bits as 11001. Key length is an important measure of a cryptosystem strength; if an attacker is attempting to break the system by trying all possible keys, adding a single bit to the key length will double the number of keys she has to test. An algorithm is considered strong if the fastest way to decrypt messages is roughly proportional to the amount of time it would take to search through all possible keys (such an effort is called a "brute-force" attack). Thus key length is important in assessing the security of a cryptosystem. An encryption algorithm with a forty-bit key—this is what could be freely exported in the 1990s—would be considered highly insecure now; modern computer processors could run through all 2^{40}—approximately 1 trillion—possible keys in a matter of minutes. One of the algorithms that the US government uses to protect information in the national security agencies has a key length of a minimum of 128 bits, making it 2^{88}—or about a billion billion billion—times as secure as an algorithm with a forty-bit key.[11]

Since 1883, it's been a tenet of cryptography that any algorithm used by more than a handful of people should be made public. The security of the system should reside solely in the secrecy of the key. Cryptographers believe that public vetting of cryptographers' algorithms is crucial; this enables outside experts to find flaws if they exist, thus establishing—or showing flaws in—the system's security.[12]

When cryptography was largely the domain of generals, diplomats, and young children, the problem of key distribution, while challenging, was possible to manage. But once the Digital Revolution made cryptography necessary for everyone, key distribution at scale became important. Whether most of us realize it or not, our days are marked by actions that require cryptography: making calls on a mobile phone (cryptography protects the calls from being overheard as they are transmitted to the base station), accepting an app update (cryptography ensures that the update is from the manufacturer), sending and receiving email (cryptography secures the communication between the sender and email provider and between the recipient and email provider), ordering an item online (cryptography ensures that your payment information is secured). To make all this work requires careful management of the cryptographic keys; doing that at scale is a very difficult problem to solve. The keys have to be shared between two entities—people or devices (or a mix of both)—that haven't met previously, and the keys must be secret from everyone else.[13]

This sounds impossible. However, in 1976, using elegant and relatively simple mathematics, Whitfield Diffie and Marty Hellman solved the problem. Their solution(s) relied on computational complexity: some computations are easy, while undoing them appears to be quite hard. Every browser, every mobile phone, and billions of other systems now implement Diffie and Hellman's idea.[14]

Let's consider one approach. Multiplication and its inverse—factorization—are a pair of computations that are easy to do, yet hard to undo. Modern computers can multiply together two 1,000-bit prime numbers p and q (a prime number is an integer divisible only by itself and one) essentially instantaneously to form their product n, where $n=pq$. It would take a modern desktop computer 6.4 quadrillion years to determine the prime factors p and q used to make this 2,000-bit n.[15]

This magical system is an example of public-key cryptography. The key, in this case, consists of two parts: a public key, in this case n, which can be known to anyone who wishes to communicate to the owner of the public key, and a private key, p and q, which is known only to the public key's owner. The system uses n to encrypt, but p and q to decrypt.[16]

Public-key systems run much more slowly than the more familiar symmetric-key encryption systems in which both sender and receiver share the same key. For this reason, public-key systems are primarily used for two purposes: transmitting keys for symmetric-key encryption and authenticating digital documents, such as software updates or banking transactions. The latter is called a digital signature, and is achieved by the sender encrypting the communication with her private key. Because this key is known only to its owner, encrypting provides proof that the communication is from the key's owner —and that the communication hasn't been tampered with during transit. The recipient can decrypt the communication using the owner's (publicly known) public key. Digital signatures are widely used for assuring authenticity. Thus, for instance, Apple's digital signature on a piece of software such as an update guarantees that the code is from Apple.

The NSA had been fighting the First Crypto War since the 1970s. In the 1990s, this war, which picked up as commercial interest in the Internet started, also began to involve the FBI. The fight was over end-to-end encryption: communications encrypted at the sender's end and decrypted at the recipient's. If a secure algorithm is properly implemented, no one but the two users can learn the message's contents. Law enforcement agencies were frantic over the possibility that encryption would render wiretaps useless. The Department of Justice decided to push first for the Communications Assistance for Law Enforcement Act (CALEA), which required that all digitally switched US networks have wiretapping capabilities built into the switches. That would give law enforcement a beachhead to exploit for the encryption problem.[17]

Congress passed CALEA in 1994. The subsequent effort to implement the law was fraught with battles over how much wiretapping capacity had to be built in. The telephone carriers and the government kept meeting in court. But more ominously, CALEA created an ongoing security problem. By requiring that wiretapping capabilities be built into telephone switches, the government created a potential security breach, and nefarious sorts took advantage of this.

Around this same time, the FBI also pressed for all encryption systems to have "key recovery" mechanisms. Despite the innocuous name, key recovery basically means a back door to get encryption keys. Communication systems are most secure if only the sender and recipient can decrypt the message. Any system for storing keys, whether held by the communications provider, the government, or a third party, weakens the system.[18]

Meanwhile, the NSA developed an encryption scheme for telephones in which keys would be split and stored with agencies of the US government. This scheme, known as Clipper, was proposed in 1993 but went nowhere fast. Industry wasn't interested in participating. Nor did Clipper solve the export issue. Other nations balked at the idea that encryption keys would be stored in the United States. Clipper was a commercial failure.[19]

Neither law enforcement agencies nor the national security community anticipated what happened next. It turned out that digital voice technology wasn't the next big new thing; the Internet was. Digital commerce was taking off. And this meant that users needed encryption to secure messages from snooping eyes, to authenticate their messages and ensure their integrity. Encryption was central to computer products—and half the market for computer equipment was outside the United States. If US companies couldn't sell computer equipment with encryption capabilities built in, other countries would. Instead of easing export controls, the government tried to bargain with computer manufacturers: products with key-recovery systems could bypass the export controls. But industry wasn't interested in key-recovery systems; it kept pressing for loosened export controls on encryption.[20]

In attempting to prevent the spread of strong encryption —encryption difficult to decrypt with current technology— the NSA and the FBI were fighting a losing battle. Industry, and to a certain extent the Department of Defense, sought strong encryption in its products (the department was increasingly relying on commercial products during this time). In response to these and other pressures, in 2000 both the United States and the European Union lifted export controls on computer and communication equipment furnished with the tools for strong end-to-end encryption. The First Crypto War had ended, and security appeared to win. In fact, though, strong encryption made its way into products only relatively slowly.

For its part, the FBI continued to campaign for key recovery. Throughout the following decade, the FBI fought an unsuccessful rearguard action against cryptography. In 2010, the FBI went public in its battle against encryption, saying that because criminals were increasingly using encrypted communications, law enforcement couldn't figure out what criminals were doing and couldn't use wiretapped evidence in court.[21]

This time around—the Second Crypto War—the FBI realized that it needed to ask for something more palatable than a "back door." In the words of FBI director James Comey, the agency wants to prevent "warrant-proof" spaces. As the FBI describes its demands, it simply wants access to decrypted communications whenever there's a court order. But instead of specifying exactly how this should be done—avoiding the fate of Clipper—the FBI has left the design to the technologists. "They're smart people in Silicon Valley," law enforcement says. "Surely those technologists can do it." Silicon Valley is skeptical. My colleague Matt Blaze, who's been developing secure computer systems since long before the term cybersecurity existed, likens the FBI's request to "Well, if we can put a man on the moon, then surely we can put a man on the sun."[22]

The FBI has changed what it says it's asking for, but changing the requirements from key recovery to access to the content of encrypted communications—sometimes called "exceptional access"—is no real change in policy. If a communication has been securely encrypted, then the only way to find out what the content says requires capturing the communication prior to encryption or after decryption—or by having a decryption key. An encryption system that provides a key to anyone but the sender or recipient will be insecure. This war is, in effect, the First Crypto War revisited.

Security experts, particularly those who have been associated with the government agencies tasked with keeping the country's most sensitive secrets, warn that the potential dangers of weakening encryption systems more than outweigh the problems such encryption systems pose for law enforcement. Months before the FBI tried to obtain a court order to force Apple to unlock San Bernardino terrorist Syed Farook's iPhone (see Chapter 1), former NSA director Mike McConnell, former secretary of the Department of Homeland Security Michael Chertoff, and Deputy Secretary of Defense William Lynn III wrote in a *Washington Post* opinion piece, "[D]espite the importance our officials attach to being able to decrypt a

coded communication under a warrant or similar legal authority . . . we believe that the greater public good is a secure
communications infrastructure protected by ubiquitous encryption at the device, server and enterprise level without building in means for government monitoring." Another former
NSA director, Michael Hayden, weighed in on the importance
of securing phones: "[W]e're probably better served by not
punching any holes into a strong encryption system—even
well-guarded holes."[23]

While the intelligence community has from time to time
complained about the problems encryption poses for investigations, the Second Crypto War appears to be largely the FBI's
battle. The exceptional access that the FBI seeks creates four
different types of security problems: it allows a retroactive compromise of prior communications; it creates greater complexity, increasing security risk; it means that weak cryptographic
algorithms last decades longer in products, undermining security for the long term; and it leaves unanswered the question
of who controls access to the key. Let's unpack these in turn.[24]

Consider what happens in a secure web browsing session, say, when a user is making flight reservations. The data
from the airline is encrypted with a symmetric key, which for
simplicity is included with the communication. But that key
has to be protected, or any eavesdropper would be able to decrypt the message. The symmetric key is therefore encrypted
with the user's public key. The recipient uses her private key
to decrypt the symmetric key, then uses the symmetric key to
decrypt the flight information. (All of this work is performed
automatically and behind the scenes by the user's browser.)
Note that the secured connection goes both ways. The airline
receives the user's credit card information encrypted with a
symmetric key protected by the airline's private key. That sim

ple model is the core idea behind the "s" in https—secure browser connections.

But this protection doesn't fully secure the connection. In cryptography we talk about "threat models." In this case, the threat is that a determined adversary might record all the communications, regardless of whether they are encrypted. If the adversary later determined the recipient's key, it could decrypt all the recorded communications. Even decades-old communications can prove useful, depending on the circumstances. Soviet diplomatic telegrams intercepted during World War II and decrypted years later, for example, led to the unmasking of Soviet spy Donald Maclean in 1951.[25]

A concept known as forward secrecy, in which new encryption keys are computed for each communication session, protects against such an attack. In this model, there is no long-term key that, once discovered, can be used to decrypt all past communications. Instead there is a new key for each communication session; when a communication is over, the key is immediately deleted. Many people, including Sony executives, now favor the use of forward secrecy for electronic communications. It's the technology behind various messaging apps, including those of Signal, WhatsApp, and Windows Off-the-Record Messaging. As of January 2017, forward secrecy is enabled on 59 percent of browsers. But in much the same way that a tape recorder can capture a voice call, forward secrecy doesn't prevent those who participate in a protected communication from storing the interchange, or information from it, themselves—and you can bet the companies do.[26]

What forward secrecy *does* protect against is someone—like an intelligence agency—vacuuming up all the communications and decrypting them by breaking one single key. Instead, the agency would have to break a key for each communication, a far more daunting process, and one unlikely to occur. Connections to Google, Facebook, and Twitter use forward secrecy by default. The kind of "exceptional access" law enforcement desires would disallow the use of forward secrecy.

The second problem with exceptional-access requirements is that they would make protocols to secure communications more complicated, rather than less. As we have seen in the example of the essentially unhackable helicopter, simplification matters in making systems secure. The more straightforward a system can be, the likelier it is that it will be, or even can be, correctly implemented.

Authenticated encryption is a way of combining two different functions—encrypting the communication and authenticating the sender—into a single step. (The latter is needed so that you know you're communicating with, say, Amazon, and not a hacker.) Doing so simplifies both security functions. That means, though, that in authenticated encryption, the same key is used for encrypting as for authenticating. The encryption key is the authentication key. If someone other than the sender has a copy of the key, the communication's authenticity can't be guaranteed. But with exceptional access, that's precisely the point: someone other than the sender will have access to the encryption key.

Authenticated encryption streamlines authentication and encryption. Exceptional access requirements would force us to abandon authenticated encryption, making us less secure, not more.

A third problem is that mandating an exceptional-access system carries long-term risks. Communication systems, whether phones or web browsers, are designed to be "backwards compatible." That's why today's smartphone can connect with the rotary phone at your grandparents' house, and why today's browsers can connect with systems set up two decades ago. But a consequence is that today's poor choices can have impact for years. Remember that forty-bit key length from the 1990s export controls? Modern browsers still have code permitting use of that forty-bit encryption in case they're connecting to a server that says "forty-bit or nothing." In 2015 researchers demonstrated that the forty-bit cryptographic option in browsers creates a security risk. Every time a secure connection—an "https" connection—is set up between a browser and a server (say, to protect credit card information or health data, or simply to keep the interchange private), there's a negotiation. The browser and server agree on a cryptographic algorithm and key for encrypting the communication session. The researchers found a way to reset the initial set of communications between the browser and server to make it appear that the server was requesting the connection use forty-bit cryptography. The result: the connection between the server and the user would rely on utterly inadequate encryption. If an exceptional-access system were to be required and then found to create serious security risks, we'd see the same problem: it would still appear in systems so that the old versions that used the exceptional-access system could work.[27]

The fourth problem is a perennial one: who would control access to the encryption keys? Any centralized key storage facility would have to satisfy the needs of multiple law enforcement agencies and multiple governments, and yet be available for immediate response. These requirements introduce great operational complexity, high costs, and, most important, massive risks, for the key repository would be a centralized target of great riches. It would literally hold the keys to the kingdom. This is not a role that private industry has shown any great interest in pursuing.

Could the government do this instead? In the United

States, one might expect a federal agency to be a key holder. But it's difficult to imagine a workable solution once a communication crosses borders—say, a communication between Germany and the United States. Who stores the keys for a communication then? If the US government has a key that enables it to read the communication, wouldn't the German government want one also? And do both have to agree in order for a communication to be decrypted? What about a communication from Chile to China that uses a service based in the United States, such as WhatsApp? The massive political complexity is outweighed only by the technical complexity that such an arrangement would produce. During the First Crypto War, other nations did not buy into the US key-escrow system; it's hard to imagine that they would do so this time round.[28]

The FBI's vision of exceptional access is not like a helicopter communication system, narrowly constrained in its use. Exceptional-access requirements make technically complex demands of encryption systems. Such complexity increases the chance for errors.

Few technologists believe a secure exceptional-access system can be built to work on a national scale. If the system were built, it would present severe risks, and they would remain so long after use of the system itself was discontinued. In 1996, a study by the National Academy of Sciences recommended that the government explore an escrowed encryption system for its own use. This never happened. Yet the lack of a large-scale working system hasn't stopped law enforcement from advocating exceptional-access solutions.[29]

I've mentioned authentication several times now. In many transactions, authentication is so basic that we don't even see it happening.

Consider the Navajo code talkers, American Indians who used their native language to transmit messages for the Marines in the Pacific during World War II. Several factors made the Navajo language perfect for the role. The language has a complex structure, with verbs made up of a verb stem combined with multiple prefixes indicating the type of action, subject, and tense. The code replaced words used during battle with code words in Navajo: America was "Ne-he-mah" (Our Mother), Torpedo Plane was "Tas-chizzie" (Swallow), Fighter Plane was "Da-he-tih-hi" (Hummingbird), and so on. But the most important part of the code wasn't anything about the language itself, but who had access to it.[30]

Relatively few people, either in the United States or abroad, spoke Navajo, let alone fluently. In prior battles, English-speaking Japanese soldiers had successfully deceived Allied soldiers by transmitting radio orders that unsuspecting Americans thought came from their own commands. The difficulty of Navajo, and the language's geographic isolation in the southwestern United States, meant that there were no Japanese or Germans fluent in the language.[31]

Navajo code talkers frequently arrived with initial assault waves so that orders could be quickly transmitted to the front. On the island of Saipan, lead troops of US Marines moved forward after the Japanese had pulled back overnight. The troops soon fell under friendly fire, and their calls to headquarters failed to stop the shelling—headquarters ignored what it thought was a Japanese trick. The next time the forward troops radioed in, headquarters asked for a Navajo code talker. The code talker transmitted the same message, but in code. The shelling stopped. Headquarters trusted the code talker, not because of what he said, but because of how he said it. He spoke as only a native speaker of Navajo could.

In so doing, he authenticated himself and his unit to headquarters.[32]

Authentication is basic to human transactions. We pay
the clerk in the convenience store because he is the person
behind the counter; we obey the woman in the dark blue uni-
form because her outfit denotes police. Sometimes we place so
much trust in certain kinds of institutions that we fail to realize that some part of the authentication mechanism has gone
missing. That's exactly what happened to the international
banking system in 2016. The result: $81 million was stolen
from Bangladesh's central bank.

This was not the first case of electronic bank theft, but it
was the first where the thieves pretended to be the bank. Previous thefts involved stealing customers' credentials and then
creating fake accounts, fake cards, and so on. This time, though,
the thieves used the credentials of the Bangladesh central bank
to authenticate itself to the bank's SWIFT terminal. Using malware that successfully undermined backup systems—and working over the weekend, so that messages querying the transactions were not seen until it was too late—the hackers ordered
transfers of almost a billion dollars to accounts in the Philippines, Sri Lanka, and other Asian nations. The bank eventually
managed to stop most of the transfers, but not the $81 million
delivered to the accounts of casinos in the Philippines, most of
which is unlikely to be recovered.[33]

Since the point of SWIFT is to provide an efficient and
secure network for the transfer of funds, SWIFT had assumed
that banks used secure authentication mechanisms. That turned
out not to be the case for the Bangladesh central bank—or
a number of other banks in the SWIFT network. SWIFT responded by updating its security requirements, including the
use of multifactor authentication to access the network. Multi-

factor authentication is a way to control access to a resource—a computer account, say, or email—by requiring several different factors. For example, a system might combine something you know (a password), something you have (some type of security token), and something you are (a fingerprint). ATM bank withdrawals require multifactor authentication: your bank card and a PIN. Of course, if you're foolish enough to write your PIN on the bank card, you've now collapsed the security into a single factor. Anyone who steals your card has both.[34]

Because user names and passwords are easy to steal, SWIFT should have insisted on multifactor authentication for banks long ago. Of course, multifactor authentication alone cannot offer 100 percent protection from network-based theft. The system may be subject to unknown vulnerabilities, and insider attacks are a risk, especially in organizations like banks or intelligence agencies, where the data is so exceedingly precious. But shoring up the weakest links—and single-factor authentication is certainly one of them—is crucial.

Silicon Valley has long used multifactor authentication solutions. When I began working at Sun Microsystems in 1999, I was given a small hardware token—a device slightly larger than a business card—that I used to log in to the company's network remotely. Each time I wanted to log in, I would type a password on the token. The network would respond by generating a six-digit number, which I then typed in to the login screen on my laptop. Without the token, I couldn't connect. (An impish family member, who thought I was traveling too much, once hid my token, causing great frustration until I found the device.)

I have already discussed one of the simplest, and now most common, types of multifactor authentication: SMS codes sent to cellphones. In 2011, when smartphones were not yet in wide use (only two-fifths of Americans and one-fifth of Western Europeans had them), this was an excellent solution. But text messages are just not that secure; they can be intercepted or redirected. Or a smooth-talking hacker might convince the phone company to switch where the authenticating texts go. Unlikely? It happened to Black Lives Matter activist DeRay Mckesson, whose Twitter account was hacked to tweet messages favoring Donald Trump. A smartphone can provide a more secure solution through an app. The site sends a notification to the smartphone app, which calculates a response. The user then transmits this response back to the site. That's how Google Authenticator, the multifactor authentication system I use for logging in to my webhosting service, works.[35]

Duo, a Michigan startup, provides a variety of tools for secure login: SMS codes (less secure), push (when the user seeks to log in to an account, the authentication system sends a notification to the phone; the user taps, and that confirms she is the one logging in), and mobile passcodes (which, like Google Authenticator, calculate a code to use for login). Duo enables system administrators to use context to protect against unauthorized logins (for example, disallowing logins from Russia). Duo's login process is simple and fast, which is important. Facebook's software engineers use a tool from Duo to securely log in to their development servers to write and submit code. Programmers have little patience and will find workarounds if a process is complicated. The good news? Duo is a success at Facebook.

Duo's multifactor app pleases some of the most security-focused people on the planet, but the company didn't build their solution for that 1 percent. Instead, they built it to arm the everyday users—the owners and workers at hair salons and auto repair shops. Jon Oberheide, Duo's cofounder and chief technology officer, explained, "Only banks and hospitals had that stuff. [But] what are the problems you see today? Because small companies will see [those problems] in five years." Duo's customers include universities, medical centers, retail, media —big institutions and small ones.[36]

US government agencies, too, are adopting smartphone multifactor solutions for authentication. Some agencies with covert operators overseas particularly like this authentication method. Using consumer smartphones to enable secure logins provides agents with protections while hiding them in plain sight.[37]

Smartphones are an extremely useful method for authenticating ourselves. Even so, often phones are the way people access online accounts. In that case, the phone can't serve as a second security factor, and another one must be found. Fortunately, these exist in the form of a small device that can be carried on a keychain. Using phones for secure login could rescue us from much of the mess created by the ease with which login credentials—typically passwords—are stolen. But that's only true if the phone itself is secure; if the phone can be hacked to access the data on it, the phone is no longer secure as an authentication device.[38]

Law enforcement isn't the only group wanting access to unlocked phones. Smartphones, and the information on them, are very attractive to criminals. Thieves sell stolen phones—there is a big overseas market—and may use the data on the phones for identity theft. As one British phone provider said, a smartphone is a "digital 'Swiss Army knife.'" They hold the minutiae of our lives: whom we call and when, where we've been (the phones often store—for years—a very precise trajectory of our travels), our text messages, email, photos, data about

our exercise habits, as well as account information (financial
and otherwise). We increasingly use smartphones as credit cards,
and they are currently more secure than the plastic version.[39]

In an experiment to track what happens to stolen phones,
the security company Symantec purposefully "lost" fifty smartphones in New York City, Washington, Los Angeles, San Francisco, and Ottawa. Symantec tracked what the finders did with
the phones, what apps were activated, and their location. The
test phones were primed with interesting-looking apps: social
networking, webmail, private pictures, human resources cases
and salaries, corporate email. The good news is that half the
finders tried to return the phones (Symantec had entered the
"owner's" phone number and email address in the Contacts
app). The bad news is that nine of ten finders accessed personal information on the phone, while eight of ten accessed
business apps.[40]

With this kind of risk, it seems like a no-brainer for individual and corporate users to secure their phones. Security
protects the data. Apple, for instance, introduced default lock
times on their phones. Users can unlock their screens through
a finger swipe pattern (easy for someone else to guess from
the smudges left on the phone), a fingerprint (law enforcement can force a user to provide the fingerprint to unlock the
phone), or a PIN. Users can control what technique they use
for unlocking—and thus how secure the lock is—and the
amount of time before an inactive phone locks. Early on, manufacturers had ways to unlock phones. But Apple sought to
make the devices more secure, which in the company's view
meant that only the user could unlock her phone—and beginning with iOS 8, that's the case.

The fact that phones automatically lock works as a deter-
rent against theft. A locked phone is a useless phone. Thieves

stole 2 million US phones in 2013, down from 3 million in 2012. Apple credits that drop to its Find My iPhone app, which lets a user locate their missing phone and lock it, and even sends messages to the person who "found" it; this feature has been quite effective at reducing iPhone theft. Android added a similar feature shortly afterwards. Adding an automatic Activation Lock, which prevents the thief from shutting off Find My iPhone as long as the phone is locked, helps even more.[41]

Find My iPhone doesn't obviate the need for encryption. Some thieves turn off a stolen phone and ship it out of the country before turning it back on. That prevents Find My iPhone from working. There's also black market software to circumvent the Find My iPhone feature. Preventing the theft of phones and protecting the information on them are related—but they're not the same thing![42]

When Apple introduced the iPhone in 2007, the company faced an important choice. Consumers would carry the iPhone with them everywhere, and so the device could have great value in tracking users, finding their shopping preferences, anticipating their needs, and advertising to them. Would Apple leverage this information to increase its profits? Or would it protect its users' privacy?

For Apple, the ability to access this information presented a new opportunity, and a new potential business strategy. Until this point, Apple had primarily been a hardware company. While Apple certainly produces the software necessary to run its hardware, including the Apple OS and iOS, it is fundamentally a hardware company with great software. The focus on hardware puts Apple in sharp contrast with Microsoft, which had demonstrated decades ago that the smart money was in developing software. Apple's business model also contrasted with that of the new data-driven companies, notably Google and Facebook, which derive their profits from the services they provide (or, more precisely, from the ads that appear alongside these services).

This difference in perspectives meant that the various giants of Silicon Valley had somewhat different takes on customer privacy. Apple doesn't need to know whether its customers prefer burritos to pizza or Beyoncé to Coltrane, so long as those customers can obtain those burritos or pizza, Beyoncé or Coltrane seamlessly off their platforms. For a company like Facebook, in contrast, such information is the core currency that drives the advertisements that sustain them.

In 2008, Apple doubled down on privacy. Starting that year, Apple began increasing the security protections on its phones. The new security features protected the data on the phone both from outside attackers and from systems legitimately on the phone. We tend to call the first set of protections security and the second privacy, although the line between the two blurs. Apple achieved these privacy protections largely through a combination of "sandboxing," which keeps enclaves of information separate, and giving users control over use of that data. Thus, for example, the user gets to decide whether an app has access to the phone's Location Services. Apple's well-known penchant for simplicity presented users with transparency in making their choices.

One reason that Apple pursued this path is that the company wanted its phones to be used in the workplace. Corporate users, in general, demand more security than individual consumers. Apple designed its phones so that they could be wiped of data quickly if lost or stolen. Apple developed a hierarchy of keys: keys that encrypted files, and keys that encrypted those keys. The iOS 3 security system relied on overwriting the base encryption key (the key that encrypts all the others). But this solution didn't take care of an underlying problem: Apple knew the base key and so had access to all data. A system in which the parent corporation, Apple, has access to all data is neither private nor secure.

For the iOS 5 operating system, released in 2011, Apple developed a more complex security system. There was still one key on the disk, which Apple could access to decrypt some files. But more sensitive files—email, the address book, and so on—were encrypted using a key that entangled the user's PIN with the phone's hardware key. Apple could not decrypt those files. By iOS 8, Apple had further reduced the chance that anyone other than the user could access data from a locked phone. Someone would need a key—again an entanglement of the user's PIN and the phone's hardware key—to unlock 90–95 percent of the phone's data. In other words, data on the phone —photos, files, iMessages—could only be decrypted through knowing the user's PIN, a key to which Apple had no access. Apple could, however, access any phone data that happened to also be stored in the iCloud. With iOS 9, Apple added yet more protections, including time delays between successive tries of the PIN and erasing the phone's data after ten bad tries.

Android's Marshmallow operating system followed suit, providing encryption for users' phone data. Even so, the privacy protections on the phones are not equal. For one thing, not all vendors of Android phones implement the encryption —and not all of those that do, do so properly. Furthermore, because nearly all Android users are signed in to a Google account, any data from a Google app is automatically stored at Google.[43]

Law enforcement's deep desire to get around these protections is the conflict at the heart of the Second Crypto War.

From iOS 8 and Marshmallow on, Apple and Android screen locks ensure, by default, that phone data is encrypted whenever the screen is locked—and that only the user can unlock the phone's contents. WhatsApp's billion users get secure messaging by default. When defaults favor security, everyone ends up with protection: good guys, dumb bad guys, and smart bad guys.

Law enforcement faced a choice between deterring crime (by limiting the value of stolen phones) and fighting crime (by having access to the information on the phones). Which way did the FBI go? In 2012, the FBI recommended that mobile phones be password-protected. In 2014, the bureau removed that advice from its website. This is exactly the wrong way to think about securing society.[44]

Syed Farook's phone had Apple's iOS 9 operating system installed. The FBI hoped that unlocking the phone would reveal where Farook and his wife had been during an eighteen-minute gap that law enforcement hadn't been able to fill in. Had they met with conspirators? The FBI wanted Apple to create an "update" for Farook's iPhone that would remove the slowdown between PIN attempts and the data erasure after ten tries. That would allow investigators to pursue a brute-force entry, in which they would try PINs until the phone unlocked. The FBI argued that, because the update would be tailored to work on Farook's phone and would be fully under Apple's control, the security of other phones would be unaffected. Apple believed otherwise. Accommodating the FBI would imperil the security of any iPhone with the same operating system and even worse, the security to the critical gatekeeping process for authorizing updates. Either would be catastrophic to iPhone security.[45]

When the FBI asked Apple to supply an update to undo the security protections on Farook's phone, law enforcement's message was explicit: this case was about opening one particular phone, not about setting precedent. But Apple's CEO Tim Cook objected, "Once created, the technique could be used over and over again, on any number of devices."[46]

Weeks later, the FBI director acknowledged that the FBI had "lots" of other locked iPhones it wanted Apple to open. At the time, the Manhattan district attorney's office had another 175 locked phones in its possession. The number of phones to be unlocked is substantially higher now. Between October and December 2016, the FBI received 1,200 locked phones for forensic analysis that it couldn't open; it is unlikely, though, that many of the investigations involve terrorism. Cook was right —and when there are lots of phones to open, there's high risk that something will go wrong. To understand why this is so, we need to explore Apple's update mechanism.[47]

When a user instructs her iPhone to update, the iPhone sends an Apple authorization server—directly or via iTunes— the device's unique ID, hashes of the software the phone is requesting, and a random number. (The last is used to prevent a "replay attack" of resending this "update"—for example, sending update iOS 9.2 when the phone is now at iOS 9.3.) The authorization server checks the device ID to determine if the update is appropriate for that model of iPhone. Then Apple signs the request—a "blob" consisting of the device ID, the hashes, and the random number—with Apple's private key. When the iPhone receives this, the device verifies that the authorization came from Apple (it does so using Apple's public key). This check prevents malware from slipping in. Then the iPhone installs the software. Right now, Apple sends out updates just a few times a year. Only a small group of highly vetted and trusted people are involved in preparing and validating Apple's update mechanism.[48]

The "security-undoing" updates that law enforcement sought would modify crucial aspects of this mechanism. By using the mechanism of the phone-unique ID, this law enforcement "update" would still particularize the update to the phone designated by the search warrant. But because of the danger involved in this law enforcement "update"—undoing Apple's carefully designed security protections—one wouldn't expect Apple to use an automated updating process, such as the one described above. A more likely scenario is that Apple would have a lawyer examine each court order, and then an engineer—a person—would install the toxic "update." The engineer wouldn't be doing anything fancy; she would just authorize the same signing process described above once the lawyer says "go ahead." Having a person present to do the update controls the process's use, so it's critical. But this means more people have access to the authorization server and its critical gatekeeping role. And this process will happen not a few times a year, but as many as tens of thousands of times annually.[49]

There's another problem as well. It's not possible to undo the security protection of a single iPhone without recording that knowledge. For one thing, Apple itself needs records of how this security-undoing update works. And if information from the phone were useful, say, in identifying another suspect who faced criminal prosecution, the government might have to disclose to the court how it obtained the evidence. The more people who knew how Apple broke into the phone— including the defense attorneys and their consultants—the greater the chance that this information would leak, imperiling the security of all iPhones. The only truly safe way for Apple to prevent public knowledge of how it hacked into a phone would be for the company to smash the device after removing the data and destroy all records of how it obtained the data. But that's not really feasible. And—needless to say—such a solution would not be palatable to the criminal justice system.[50]

The insider threat from developing such knowledge is also very real. Apple would be involving many more people in the phone-update process. Maybe a rogue request comes from someone pretending to be the Las Vegas district attorney, or maybe it comes from a rogue employee at Apple (if the FBI, CIA, and NSA can suffer from rogue employees, then so can Apple). The result? Maybe a phone that shouldn't get a security-undoing update does. A phone that an unfriendly government, a criminal organization, or a business competitor wants to examine receives a signed security update from Apple that enables the government, criminal group, or competitor to probe the smartphone and read its data. The phone itself can be taken during a customs inspection or a meeting in which all electronic devices are kept outside the room. One act of neglect, or one careless or cheating employee, and the security of all Apple products would be deeply, perhaps irrevocably, damaged.[51]

But far more dangerous than any of these risks is the threat to Apple's signing key. If Apple's signing key were coopted, Apple devices could not be trusted, period. Too far a stretch? That's what happened in Stuxnet (see Chapter 3). Stolen private keys allowed signed malware to masquerade as legitimate, and thus to be installed in the Natanz systems.[52]

Why then is it safe for the government to either develop or purchase hacking tools to break into the iPhone but not for Apple to do so? The answer is quite simple. A vulnerability in a single iOS version can be patched. But were Apple to develop ways to open its secure phones, its process for doing so—and for signing software—would become potentially vulnerable. And that would put the security of all of Apple's devices at risk.

Given the value of the software to criminal organizations and spying agencies, leaks are absolutely inevitable. Just consider the 2013 Snowden disclosures, or the 2017 WikiLeaks dump of CIA hacking tools. We have seen one highly sophisticated and capable adversary disrupt the 2016 US presidential campaign. Could Apple withstand a prolonged attack by a nation-state on its update process? I would not agree to that bet. That's a security risk simply too high to take.

In the 1990s, export controls were limiting US use of products with strong encryption—manufacturers were loath to produce a version with strong encryption for domestic use and with weak encryption for use abroad—but that didn't stop other nations from obtaining cryptography. A 1999 study by George Washington University found 167 encryption systems produced abroad that included strong cryptography. That means that, while the export controls thwarted buyers of US systems from simply flipping a switch to turn on strong encryption, those determined to encrypt their communications had plenty of products to choose from.[53]

None of the cryptographic systems, however, could be described as easy-to-use consumer products. The closest approximation to a consumer product might have been one my colleague Whitfield Diffie (the coinventor of public-key cryptography) and I relied on in the mid-1990s. We didn't have anything particularly secret to discuss; Whit just likes testing encryption tools.

Each of us had an encryption device about the size and shape of a video cassette, which we connected to our desk phones. The box had a screen on which a combination of six digits and letters would appear after our call was connected. The very first thing we'd do after we initiated the encryption was to check that we had the same set of six digits and letters on our two screens, Whit reading the first three to me, I reading the second set to him. The set was generated from the encryption key we used for our conversation—a key that was unique to our communication—and that set provided the evidence that no one was listening in.[54]

If an eavesdropper, Eve, were listening in to our conversation, she'd be decrypting Whit's communications, then reencrypting them to me, and also decrypting my communications and reencrypting them to Whit. Eve would have an encryption key for her call with Whit and another one for the call with me. These two encryption keys would be different, and thus the set of digits and letters that would show up on our respective screens would not match. When Whit and I read the three digits and numbers out to each other and confirmed we were seeing the same set, we were confirming the security of our call. There was no middleman listening in.

Our device was expensive and complicated; the system spent 97 percent of its computational effort transforming our voices from an analog signal into a digital one, and only 3 percent on encrypting the signal. Twenty years of progress in technology have made all the difference. Mobile phones far smaller than our encryption boxes now perform that audio-to-digital conversion. Thus, contemporary apps encrypt communications at a fraction of the cost of our clunky, hand-built system. That change in technology, combined with the removal of export controls in 2000, enabled strong decryption to be deployed in consumer devices and applications. Those protections first began to be deployed in the late 2000s, but they took off with a vengeance post-Snowden.

Signal, for example, is an app that provides end-to-end encrypted group, text, picture, and video messages and encrypted voice calls between its users; it works on both Android and iOS. Signal's approach is based purely on security and privacy: it uses forward secrecy, doesn't collect communications metadata, and doesn't back up users' messages to Google or iCloud when they back up their phones. Just as with the encryption system that Whit and I used in the 1990s, users have to verify a security code at the beginning of a conversation to ensure there's no eavesdropper. Signal, though, provides a more user-friendly system than the one Whit and I shared. The sender and recipient receive two words to exchange instead of a random string of six letters and numbers. Signal's code is also open-source, making it available for inspection. Signal has been publicly vetted, and it's trusted.

In many ways, the messaging app WhatsApp, which added end-to-end encryption to its messaging, voice calls, and video applications, has Signal beat. The app uses strong encryption—it implements Signal's technology but with different usability choices—and it works for the vast majority of smartphones. With a billion users, that's fantastic news for security.[55]

But WhatsApp's story also reveals tradeoffs companies make when balancing users' security needs with their demand for convenience. If a user gets a new SIM card—which happens monthly in some parts of the world—her public/private encryption key pair changes. It's like she's a new person to the system. How should her contacts handle that? WhatsApp aims for high reliability. So the message goes through and then WhatsApp tells the sender—if she has turned on the notifications setting—that the recipient's phone has changed. This creates a security risk; without reauthentication happening first, the communication could be being sent to an eavesdropper. In this situation, Signal only delivers the message after checking with the user about reauthenticating the recipient.

And that's the point. Signal's users are keenly concerned about security, and are willing to put up with some unreliability. WhatsApp's users are more focused on reliability. Available in over fifty languages, WhatsApp is an international hit. It vastly improves the security for almost all of its users.[56]

Iranians prefer Telegram, a Berlin-based messaging app that claims to provide strong security. A closer examination, however, raises doubts. In Telegram, end-to-end encryption is not the default setting. Nor has the company made its "unique, custom protocol" for cryptography public. That's a red flag to security researchers, who distrust an encryption system they can't probe for weaknesses. But 100 million people use the system monthly, and jihadists have flocked to this non-US-based service. Whether Telegram provides them the security they expect is unknown.[57]

Some algorithms protect communications content, but as we learned in Chapter 1—and will see in more detail in Chapter 5—law enforcement and intelligence officials can find transactional information (the who and when of a connection) revelatory, even without access to content. Even if your browser is using forward secrecy on all its connections, your ISP knows to which site you're connecting. The website you're visiting learns your Internet protocol (IP) address—and, often, enough other data to uniquely identify your machine, and possibly your name.[58]

As an alternative, some users have sought out, and some security analysts recommend, online anonymity. There are many types of anonymity a user might seek: she might not want her ISP to know she's visiting a site on growing pot at home, or she might not want the site to know how to find her (an IP address is useful for tracing a user). The onion router (Tor), for

example, was developed at the US Naval Labs to provide online anonymity; routing information—where the user wants
to go—is encased, like an onion, in layers of encryption that
are unwrapped as the data travels from the user to the site and
back again.[59]

There are many legitimate and important reasons for
users to seek online anonymity. These reasons can be as mundane as a teenager checking out birth control or a potential
employee checking out a new company's benefits, or as high-
stakes as someone in an abusive situation exploring her options or providing a tip to an investigator's hotline. Of course,
there are also other reasons a user might want online anonymity: for instance, engaging in drug dealing, or purchasing stolen credit card information. Tor prevents the website you're
visiting from knowing your IP address even as you get to see
the site. And Tor also prevents your ISP from knowing which
site you're accessing.

Anonymization tools are also essential for people in sensitive jobs to carry out their duties. Law enforcement uses anonymization tools when conducting work undercover—it's difficult to impersonate a hacker or a child pornographer when
your IP address reveals you to be coming from fbi.gov. Military personnel working abroad use Tor to connect back home
to keep their identity safe from snooping ISPs. Human-rights
workers and journalists operating in dicey situations similarly
wish to keep their identity and activities hidden. Even people
performing tasks that are not dangerous but are still confidential, such as business analysts conducting research on areas for
investment, may find it advantageous to hide their identities.

Having many anonymous online users is beneficial for
those who depend on it: Tor's cloak covers best when a large
number of people are using it. As the Tor people say, "Ano-

nymity loves company." Without wide use, Tor's government users might as well wear a sign advertising, "I work for the US government doing secret business."[60]

As we move more of our lives into the online world, people have more and more reasons to encrypt. New products have followed. A 2016 study found 865 encryption products available worldwide, 546 of them originating outside the United States. Not all of these are secure, or serve a large audience, or are easy to use. But the sheer number of products shows the difficulty that a US law to control encryption would encounter. A US encryption statute might govern products built or sold in the United States, but it won't prevent products from being developed overseas. And while US law might be able to control a piece of hardware like the iPhone, the ready availability of encrypted apps makes it nearly impossible to prevent their proliferation. Regardless of US controls, criminals and terrorists will be able to obtain encryption products that the government cannot access. But the people who have legitimate needs to secure their information will only have access to the deliberately weakened systems—giving bad guys easier ways into their data. This makes no sense.[61]

During the height of the First Crypto War, the pivotal study issued by the National Academy of Sciences concluded that "on balance, the advantages of more widespread use of cryptography outweigh the disadvantages." The security risks have grown since, in ways that are more threatening than we imagined even a year ago. End-to-end cryptography and secured phones will not solve the cybersecurity problem. They won't prevent DDoS attacks, and they are only partially useful in case of an insider attack. They won't stop an extremely skilled antagonist. But their use will make attacks more difficult and slow down the attackers; in many instances, that may be "good enough."[62]

End-to-end encrypted devices and secured smartphones will make law enforcement's job more difficult. But it may be that the wealth of investigative tools that law enforcement found at its fingertips over the last decade and a half was an unusual situation, not to be repeated. As former NSA director Michael Hayden put it, "What we're arguing about preserving may be the aberration." He pointed out that fifteen years ago we were not putting all our private information and histories of our locations on our phones. Hayden added, "We may actually be returning to the state of nature we had before." Law enforcement will have to once again learn to function in a world without saturation knowledge.[63]

5

Investigations in the Age
of Encryption

I n 1992, the FBI's Advanced Telephony Unit issued a dire
warning: law enforcement was on the verge of losing its
ability to listen in. They predicted that within three years,
encryption would render 40 percent of all criminal wiretaps incomprehensible. But the FBI could not have been more
wrong. Encryption gained few followers in the 1990s.[1]

In 2010, the FBI once again warned that its ability to
conduct investigations was being curtailed, this time by the
complexities presented by social network sites, peer-to-peer
communications systems, and—yes—encryption. According
to the FBI, its wiretapping abilities were "going dark." But,
once again, the claim was a bit surprising. As Edward Snowden's
2013 disclosures about NSA surveillance made clear, the intelligence agency had developed strategies for conducting surveillance across the globe. With the Snowden revelations in
the headlines, the FBI went quiet about going dark.[2]

This was the background against which the FBI attempted
to get a court order to force Apple to decrypt a suspected ter-

rorist's phone (see Chapter 1). FBI director James Comey accused Silicon Valley of promoting encryption as a "marketing pitch" without regard to the consequences for public safety or law enforcement. The 2015 San Bernardino terrorist attack appeared to give the FBI a winning court case: a horrific crime, a phone that might provide leads on coconspirators, and a private corporation that would not cooperate. The situation did not work out exactly as the FBI anticipated.[3]

By 2016, the question of smartphone security was no longer abstract. The public saw the issue in terms of their devices, which held their messages, email, photos, and bank account information. Even though the Apple-FBI dispute involved a terrorism case, public opinion did not favor law enforcement's position. Favoring security over access, a number of retired senior intelligence officials quite publicly took Apple's side in the fight.[4]

In less than twenty years, the Digital Revolution has transformed the way law enforcement conducted investigations. Communications now travel in different, and often more confusing, ways than they did two decades ago. The volume of communications has increased tremendously, accompanied by more detailed metadata. Digital photos, for instance, typically include the time and GPS location of when and where they were taken. Investigators—the NSA, the FBI, the Secret Service (which probes financial crimes), the Drug Enforcement Administration (DEA), and state and local police—have adapted to these new realities in various ways, with varying abilities. These differing competencies go some way toward explaining why former intelligence officials embraced the general use of end-to-end encryption and secured phones, while domestic law enforcement pointedly did not. But more than this, the split between intelligence and law enforcement in the

Apple case mirrored the different ways that these communities had responded to the Digital Revolution in general.

The NSA is a signals-intelligence agency. Signals-intelligence agencies listen in; that's their job. They may physically tap communication lines, pluck signals out of the air through radio receivers, or place satellites in space. They seek to undo communication protections, ideally in a way that ensures that they—and no one else besides the sender and receiver—can make sense of intercepted messages. As communications technologies change, interception methods must change as well.

Two decades ago, the NSA faced serious challenges. With the end of the Cold War, the agency had seen massive budget cuts, just at the moment that changes in communications technology were complicating its efforts. Telecommunications companies replaced overseas radio transmissions, which were easy to intercept, with fiber-optic cables, which were not. Nations increased their use of cryptography. Acquiring and analyzing signals became much more difficult. The arrival of digital communications exacerbated the problem. The Digital Revolution meant many more communications, arriving much more quickly, and in multiple formats. Instead of simply intercepting telephone calls, telegrams, and faxes, the NSA had to deal with email, instant messaging, files, attachments, webpages, videos, and games, all in varying formats. And all the while, engineers kept designing even more new communications schemes.

"Signals intelligence is in a crisis," said one Washington insider. By the late 1990s there was talk of NSA "going deaf."[5]

The NSA had faced challenges before. In the early decades of the Cold War, Soviet communications traveled via high-frequency radio; the United States built intercept stations around the periphery of the Soviet Union to capture the communications signals. But in the 1970s, radio communications switched over to microwave transmission. Microwave transmissions travel in line of sight, and if the signal was sufficiently far away, it would evade the surveillance system placed on the earth's curved surface. The intercept stations were useless.[6]

NSA signals intelligence was in trouble. Fortunately for the agency, the United States had another tool, the RHYOLITE satellite program to collect telemetry information—the "how fast" and "how high"—on Soviet missile tests. Perched in a geosynchronous orbit above the middle of the Soviet Union, RHYOLITE was in a perfect position to look down and collect microwave radio and long-distance communications traffic across the country. The NSA was able to stay in business.[7]

During this time, the agency had one success after another. It predicted the North Vietnamese Tet offensive in 1968, learned and passed on the inner thoughts of Soviet leadership during negotiations on the 1972 Strategic Arms Limitation Treaty, and anticipated the 1979 Soviet invasion of Afghanistan ten days before it began. But by the late 1990s, facing massive increases in the "3 V's" of electronic communications—volume, velocity, and variety—the NSA was once again in trouble. Its deputy director of operations said the agency was a "shambles." The NSA didn't foresee India's first round of nuclear tests in 1998. During the 1999 Kosovo war, the signals-intelligence agency had to cut back on normal data traffic to be able to send NATO bombers mission-critical information. The agency was unable to process information quickly enough to please its customers.[8]

These and other crises forced the NSA to adapt. The post-9/11 war on terrorism brought generous funding for intelligence agencies. The agency hired large numbers—the exact number is classified, but is in the thousands—of computer scientists to build the tools to handle the flood of digital data. The agency's highly secretive Office of Tailored Access Operations (TAO), in existence since at least 1998, engages in sophisticated hacking operations, including implanting spyware into the hard drives of 80,000 systems around the world. Such spyware compromises a system's security, perhaps by leaking encryption keys or changing parameters to weaken the algorithm. With TAO "implants," NSA collected intelligence on Al Qaeda operatives as the United States sought Osama bin Laden. NSA surveillance enabled the precise targeting involved in the Natanz operation in Iran (see Chapter 3). NSA's intimate knowledge of North Korean networks allowed the United States to identify the nation as Sony's attacker (see Chapter 1).[9]

By the time of the Snowden disclosures in 2013—which revealed the existence of the TAO—the agency had a deserved reputation for intercepting and analyzing encrypted communications from around the world. Reports of TAO's capabilities sufficiently worried the Russians that they reportedly temporarily switched to using manual typewriters to protect communications of high-level officials.[10]

Easy access to encryption capabilities makes accessing content harder. But no one now says that the NSA is going deaf. Sometimes the NSA breaks into systems and collects information before it is encrypted, sometimes the agency tampers with equipment or algorithms to get around the cryptography, and sometimes the NSA relies on alternate information, such as communications metadata, to substitute for content. Instead of folding up shop, the NSA gained new capabilities and new powers. Or, as former NSA director Mike McConnell observed, "From that time until now, NSA has had better 'sigint' [signals intelligence] than at any time in history." And the 2017 WikiLeaks release of CIA hacking tools showed that that agency had developed a strong set of capabilities as well.[11]

The FBI took a completely different approach to the Digital Revolution. Instead of embracing the new digital tools, the FBI tried to rein in the technology. As we have seen in Chapter 4, the FBI's various attempts to control the use of encryption through legal restrictions failed. Meanwhile the social media companies—and digital technologies in general—were creating vast pools of evidentiary information for law enforcement. Instead of finding ways to use this information, the FBI complained that the vast variety of digital communications was making its job harder. In 2011, FBI general counsel Valerie Caproni told Congress, "The number of ways in which we communicate has exploded. . . . The advances . . . have made it exponentially more difficult for law enforcement to execute court-authorized wiretaps." Communications at Twitter, Facebook, MySpace, and the virtual reality platform Second Life were unencrypted, but "it takes time to engineer a solution," Caproni complained. The FBI apparently not only wanted access to the data, but wanted that data brought to them on a platter.[12]

In 2014 Apple moved forward with its plans to secure the iPhone. Two years later, the FBI went to the courts over the San Bernardino terrorist case, arguing that a 1789 law, the All Writs Act, compelled the Silicon Valley company to create software to undo the iPhone's security protection. A few weeks later, the director presented the FBI's position in Congress. Congressman Darrell Issa, who'd once run a company making car antitheft devices, focused on the efforts the FBI had made to unlock the device.

MR. ISSA: Did you receive the source code from Apple? Did you demand the source code?

MR. COMEY: Did we ask Apple for their source code? I don't—not that I'm aware of. . . .

MR. ISSA: Okay. Well, let's go through the 5C running iOS 9. Does the 5C have a nonvolatile memory in which all of the encrypted data and the selection switches for the phone settings are all located in that encrypted data?

MR. COMEY: I don't know.

MR. ISSA: Well, it does. . . . So that means that you can, in fact, remove from the phone all of its memory, all of its nonvolatile memory, its disk drive, if you will, and set it over here and have a true copy of it that you could conduct infinite number of attacks on. Let's assume that you can make an infinite number of copies once you make one copy, right?

MR. COMEY: I have no idea.

MR. ISSA: . . . If you haven't asked that question, the question is, how can you come before this Committee and before a Federal judge, and demand that somebody else invent something, if you can't answer the questions that your people have tried this?

MR. COMEY: First thing, I'm the Director of the FBI. If I could answer that question, there would be something dysfunctional in my leadership.[13]

Darrell Issa was surely not expecting to use a congressional hearing to work out the technical details of getting data off an iPhone. The congressman was probing how the FBI investigated twenty-first-century technologies. Comey's response was to claim that a 1789 law absolved it of the responsibility to solve technological questions. But the Digital Revolution isn't going away. Yet neither are the types of investigations that rely on wiretaps and locked digital phones.

Classic wiretapping is no longer the only option for investigators, whether they're looking into terrorism or more run-of-the-mill crimes. Let's begin exploring the alternatives by examining cases where encrypted communications and locked phones present the greatest impediments to law enforcement: terrorism, drug, and child pornography cases.

Terrorism cases can take the form of lone-wolf attacks, which involve one or two people acting alone, or larger, more organized attacks, like 9/11 or the 2015 attacks in Paris. It is extraordinarily difficult to prevent lone-wolf attacks. Some can be thwarted through the use of well-placed informers and monitoring known suspects, but total prevention isn't realistic in a world in which knives, guns, bomb-making materials, or even cars and trucks are available. By contrast, the planning and financing that go into large-scale attacks increase the likelihood that intelligence agencies will learn that something is in the works. Exactly *what* terrorists have in mind, however, may not be at all clear. In such cases, access to content can really be valuable. That is particularly the case with would-be terrorists participating in relatively simple plots—shootings or stabbings, for example—directed from abroad.[14]

Drug cases often involve large conspiracies and, like terrorism, have senior people who use good operations security and low-level operatives who do not. Federal investigators focus on the kingpins, often by following the money. State and local police, who conduct the vast majority of drug prosecutions, focus on low-level dealers, using them to inform on higher-ups.

(State and local police also prosecute users in large numbers; the federal government rarely does.)[15]

Child pornography presents a situation in which the crime itself has changed due to the Internet. Where photos were once exchanged in furtive dark corners in real life, child porn has now moved online. Because child porn networks so frequently require users to provide some "of your own" to join, child pornographers have been engaged in a race to the bottom, often providing live video of young children.

Easy cases, relatively speaking, occur when police are tipped off about a suspect with child porn. People who provide a tip about child porn don't tend to want anonymity, and they willingly offer police what information they have. Police go to the ISP, seeking to discover what websites the suspect is visiting. If that doesn't work, there are often other ways to figure out what the suspect is doing. One Texas investigator told me, "The majority of the time we're able to get in, either with consent [of the device owner] or with probable cause"—that is, through obtaining a search warrant. Here's where the Digital Revolution may come in handy: if police find relevant photos on the phones, they usually come stamped with time and location, helping police to identify—and protect—the victims.[16]

But the Digital Revolution complicates investigations when police start with a child porn chat room or site. Users often employ anonymization tools—typically Tor—to hide their IP address. It's difficult to grab that first thread that offers investigators a chance to unravel the identities of the site's users.

Do encryption and anonymization tools create serious problems for law enforcement investigators in these cases? Absolutely. But the Digital Revolution also opened the gates for a flood of data that created what some commentators have

called the "Golden Age of Surveillance." New forms of data—
for instance, location information and time stamps—combined
with new ways of handling this data—searching and visualiza-
tion tools—have greatly simplified the process of discovering
what suspects might be up to. By 2015, 96 percent of criminal
wiretaps involved mobile phones. In one sense, this number is
not so surprising, as by 2011, half of all voice calls used mobile
phones. And criminals tend to favor using cellphones.[17]

The challenges of encrypted communications and secured devices must be examined within this larger picture. To
do otherwise would be like complaining that Henry Ford gave
bank robbers getaway cars without acknowledging the extent
to which patrol cars transformed policing.

Real investigations have always been built out of bits and
pieces. Reflecting on his time as a prosecutor, former Secretary
of Homeland Security Michael Chertoff told me, "A lot of time
you didn't get evidence on a wiretap. We took photos, we got
witnesses, we got forensics (like fingerprints). There was metadata. I convicted a whole lot of people, putting it all together
from individual pieces of evidence."[18]

Communications metadata can show the underlying
structure of criminal and terrorist conspiracies. This metadata
is everywhere: in the bits in the cell towers that say this phone
was in this vicinity at this time, and in routers that say an email
was sent at this moment from this physical vicinity. Even negative metadata—for instance, that a phone was turned off in a
given vicinity—can benefit investigators. In France, police have
used information on when and where phones are turned off to
find criminals using stolen credit cards. Patterns that show pairs
of phones that trade off—one working only when the other is
not—can highlight the presence of terrorists or drug dealers.

A determined Beirut investigator studied the metadata associated with a complex set of cellphone calls—using purely cell ID and time-of-call data—to uncover the group that had assassinated former Lebanese prime minister Rafik Hariri through a suicide truck bombing. Through meticulous study of the phone records, the investigators uncovered all the information they needed: who led the plot, how they planned it, how they purchased the truck, and how they had practiced.[19]

Metadata is not foolproof. Cell tower information says you're within range of a tower—but the cell tower handling the call was not necessarily the one closest to the phone. Which tower handles a call depends on many factors, including local congestion, maintenance schedules, and the like. (In contrast, GPS information from a phone, such as is supplied to Google Maps, does pinpoint location.) That the cell tower is only an approximate locator matters in criminal investigations. In 2014 an Oregon court overturned a ten-year-old murder conviction because the evidence—records from a cell tower—had not proved the suspect was at the location at the time of the murder.[20]

Law enforcement also benefits from the Digital Revolution. The rise of online social networks tremendously altered what information people share about themselves and how they provide it. Postings on Facebook, Instagram, Twitter, LinkedIn, and Renren have transformed the way people connect with one another. Social media encourages users to post photographs and video, which compels other users to share their own. Over 400 hours of video are posted on YouTube every minute, which means that even the most dedicated watcher can see only a tiny fraction of what is being produced. A remarkable amount of personal information is now easily accessible in the form of bits that can be searched, found, and used.

Because people want access to their contact lists, calendars, email, and files wherever they are—and with whichever device they happen to be carrying—they store data in the cloud. Companies offering these services set storage and synching to occur automatically. And while cloud data may be encrypted, in many instances the provider's business model is to make money from "knowing the user," with the company holding a decryption key. Armed with a court order, law enforcement can almost always get access to the information in decrypted form. The popularity of US companies such as Google and Facebook makes obtaining the information much easier for US law enforcement than if the data were stored abroad.

Ephemeral conversations—a momentary discussion at someone's office door, a quick call on the phone—have migrated to electronic communications. Momentary exchanges that in the past might have dissipated into the air are now stored. Think back to Chapter 1, where I described how US Attorney Preet Bharara used a text message from Roomy Khan to Raj Rajaratnam to unravel a complex insider trading case. In its entirety, this message read: "do not buy plcm till i het guidance." Had the message been transmitted by an earlier technology—perhaps over the phone or left on an answering machine (and then deleted)—Bharara's team would not have had that crucial initial piece of evidence.[21]

One of the newer—and more unsettling—types of information now available to law enforcement is conversations overheard by smart devices. Various devices, including Amazon's Alexa, Samsung's Smart TV, and Apple's Siri, provide services by responding to voice commands. The catch is that these devices don't figure out what you want just by listening to you. Some do if the request is simple (for example, "Switch to channel 7"). Most times the device just sends the inquiry to the cloud. Fast algorithms parse your request and send a response to the device in your hand or living room. Voice-controlled smart devices work by always listening; they're the eavesdroppers you've invited in. In conjunction with British intelligence, the US Central Intelligence Agency developed malware that can be implanted on a Samsung Smart TV to do exactly that—and transmit the recorded audio, presumably to a government server. In 2016, the US director of national intelligence, James Clapper, observed, "In the future, intelligence services might use the [Internet of Things] for identification, surveillance, monitoring, location tracking, and targeting for recruitment, or to gain access to networks or user credentials."[22]

The Digital Revolution's impact on law enforcement investigations has been profound. Consider how Patrick Fitzgerald, a former US district attorney who successfully prosecuted crime bosses, the 1993 World Trade Center bombing case, and two Illinois governors, has integrated these new capabilities into his cases. When Fitzgerald was investigating the attack on the World Trade Center in the mid-1990s, he was fascinated by the information provided by phone records. "I would find defense attorneys who would say Mr. X and Mr. Y didn't know each other or never talked," Fitzgerald described, "and I would spend my evenings with phone bills trying to prove they must have talked, they must have talked lots of times."[23]

Fitzgerald knew that even without voice recordings, phone information could show the outline of what occurred. "You figured out that the one person that everyone agrees is a terrorist—maybe he's already convicted (he's not on trial)—bought urea nitrate. And you show that just before he went to buy the urea nitrate, he called the defendant. Then you said he went and bought explosive detonators, and you showed a phone record; he called the defendant. Then he went and did a surveillance; then he called the defendant." At the time (1993), this work wasn't easy. The FBI had three sets of phone records, and Fitzgerald would spend his evenings comparing them by hand. Now investigators can use an automatic tool to show the connections and a timeline—in seconds.[24]

Fitzgerald learned the value of other types of data analytics while conducting drug and gang investigations in the early 2000s. Such enforcement typically involved prosecuting a low-level participant and flipping him to get information on his dealer. The US Organized Crime Drug Enforcement Force, a national force in which Fitzgerald participated, wanted to look at data correlations. Fitzgerald resisted at first; it seemed like just so much paper pushing. But data correlations could pull out the fact that a peripheral drug dealer in Atlanta was also in Chicago and Houston—and was, in fact, a key player. This was gold. Such a data-analytic approach was new to crime fighting.[25]

The criminal justice system often lacked access to these tools. In the 2000s, Fitzgerald's office had investigated the financial industry, which was showing clear signs of trouble, yet investigators in Fitzgerald's office couldn't determine who was responsible for a fraudulent transaction simply from bank reports. A name might appear on page 300 of a report from one bank and again on page 400 of a report from another. Finding correlations and uncovering the perpetrators behind them should not have been the stuff of science fiction. With the limited means the US attorney's office had at their disposal, however, it might as well have been.[26]

By 2012, Fitzgerald's office had modern tools. Data-analytics software could pull common title insurance brokers and real estate lawyers from bank records and illuminate a pattern of problematic mortgages. Automatic tools could create a timeline of emails and phone calls alongside times of stock trades and merger announcements, information for leads to insider trading.

Fitzgerald's office obtained many of these capabilities from Palantir, an analytics company that supplied them with a data analysis framework and an easy way to search across separate databases. These databases might consist of files of crime and arrest information, field interview cards, or logs of phone calls and emails. Such capabilities are hardly startling to computer scientists, but for law enforcement they represented an entirely new world. "A lot of what we do in law enforcement is surprisingly mundane," explained Courtney Bowman, a researcher for Palantir. Mundane, yet powerful. There's legitimate wariness about the power of the tools and the possibility that they might be turned against the public. These days Palantir's workforce includes "civil liberties engineers," who ensure that the collection and use of data stay on the right side of the law, and auditing code that provides a trail for how data is collected and how it's used.[27]

Investigators can sometimes crack cases with only partial information through the power of linked databases. A Los Angeles robbery victim told police the getaway car was a gray Cadillac with a license plate that included "671." Searching databases, the police found the car's license. Several days later, they located the car, arresting its occupants as they attempted another robbery. The tools help "make sense of all the noise that's out there," said Los Angeles police chief Charlie Beck. Similarly, patterns of bank deposits and communications can expose the perpetrators at the center of a human trafficking scheme.[28]

Often communications metadata will be combined with other sources of data. Palantir researchers noted a case in which law enforcement was interested in a particular car. Police tracked the car's travel using automatic license plate readers. Checking lawfully acquired records collected from cell towers along the route, they identified a second suspect through a phone number linked to the car in question.

Data and automation can cut the costs of investigations drastically. Using a team of plainclothes officers in unmarked cars to track a suspect generally runs $275 an hour. Placing a GPS device on a suspect's car costs only $10 an hour. Using a cell signal to follow a suspect is cheaper yet: only $5.21 an hour. And the Digital Revolution provides this information—cloud data, communications metadata, location information—without encryption getting in the way. The broad availability of data caused the National Network to End Domestic Violence to conclude that victims of domestic abuse were best served by the privacy protections of strong smartphone encryption—even if that made investigations of their abusers more difficult to conduct.[29]

Of course, sometimes old-fashioned investigative techniques work just fine. A former senior FBI executive told me, "We're going back to traditional technologies ... going back to HUMINT [human intelligence]." Other national security and law enforcement officials, including former NSA director Michael Hayden, have echoed that observation. This is not surprising; policing has always relied on talking with people: victims, witnesses, suspects, nonsuspects, confidential sources. As encryption dries up some amount of wiretapping, police will have to rely on the old tried-and-true methods. They produce results.[30]

And never underestimate the power of simple solutions. Some police officers have reported that asking the criminal to unlock the phone does the trick. Others have left suspects alone in an interrogation room, with their locked phones nearby. When they can't resist the temptation to check their phone, a police officer quickly reenters to pick up the unlocked phone. Other police departments train a well-placed video camera on the screen to catch the PIN. In the United States, policy is to obtain a search warrant first: since 2013, no phone searches can happen without one. Britain's Scotland Yard employs a variation on this: waiting to arrest a criminal until he's on the phone, then swooping in and grabbing the device, swiping through the screens as someone else collars the suspect.[31]

Now that we know a little bit more about the tools law enforcement uses to conduct investigations, let's revisit how the authorities approach cases involving terrorism, drugs, and child pornography.

In a lone-wolf terrorist attack, investigation is likely to be after the fact. Law enforcement wants to know who did it—and how. In 2013, two bombs went off within thirteen seconds at the Boston Marathon's finish line. Three people were killed, and hundreds more were seriously wounded. Who did it? No one called to claim credit. But cameras nearby were busy recording. Within two days, police scanning the videos honed in on a man placing a backpack on the ground, walking away, and not turning around when a bomb went off. Shortly afterwards, the Boston police commissioner, looking at the tapes, identified the second bomber. The police published photos of the bombers; members of the public identified them. The bombers went on the run, but were quickly found after they hijacked a car with a GPS and mobile assistance system. Phones, ubiquitous video cameras, automatic license plate readers, and other surveillance systems make it very difficult for suspects to disappear.[32]

Larger conspiracies usually leave tracks, and intelligence or law enforcement may be able to conduct surveillance before an event happens. In such cases, being able to listen in can be invaluable. Yet even if police can understand the words, coded language may make it impossible to comprehend the plot. Anyone listening in to the 9/11 plotters, for example, would have heard about the "faculty of urban planning" and the "faculty of fine arts"—but had no way to deduce that these phrases referred to the World Trade Center and the Pentagon, respectively.[33]

Because terrorists are aware that encryption products may include a backdoor for US intelligence, they generally prefer home-grown solutions to those available on the open market. In 2007, Al Qaeda released its own encryption software, Mujahadeen Secrets. After the Snowden disclosures revealed the wide extent of NSA surveillance, Islamic terrorist organizations grew more distrustful of Western encryption products. They developed additional products of their own, including a messaging tool and software for mobile platforms. But since terrorist encryption systems don't face the public vetting that a system such as Tor or Signal undergoes, they are, in fact, less likely to be secure.[34]

Communications metadata can be extremely useful in terrorism cases. For example, investigators were wiretapping a German terrorist suspect when they overheard a conversation with no words or sounds. Investigators followed the SIM card from the call; even as Khalid Sheikh Mohammed, the plotter of the 9/11 attacks, kept changing phones, he continued using the card. This was the clue that eventually led to his capture in Karachi.[35]

I asked NSA deputy director Rick Ledgett about metadata's limits. "Metadata is not a substitute for content," he told me. "It can't tell you here is the plan, here's how we're going to do it. . . . It likely won't tell you the timing, again, until it's too late, when it's actually happening. And so the idea that metadata is a suitable substitute for content just doesn't track in my experience." Then Ledgett added, "But I think metadata is useful. It can tell you who's in contact with who, it can tell you when. The right kind of metadata can tell you where. You can get sequencing of activities, even if you don't know exactly what those activities are. You can get associations of people with other people or with events or with physical locations. So all those things are useful from a national security point of view."[36]

Terrorists know that metadata can give away far too much about their activities. Bin Laden's concern about the US ability to track him via his communications led the Al Qaeda leader to resort to an old message delivery system: courier. (Ironically, the United States eventually located bin Laden by tracking his courier.) At least since the mid-2000s, terrorist groups have employed a variety of encryption measures not only to obscure the content of their messages, but also to hide their very existence.[37]

Investigating drug cases bears some similarity to terrorism investigations. Drug kingpins can be quite sophisticated about encryption. The Zeta cartel in Mexico, for instance, built their own communications network, with antennas, repeaters, solar power sources—and encryption. And even when drug dealers don't encrypt their communications, they often converse in code. Chertoff said, "It's rare for people in organized crime or drug dealers [to say much]. I'm hard pressed to remember much in the way of a phone call [that said more than], 'Hey, did you get that thing I sent with the guy?' "[38]

Local dealers are turning to encryption, too, saying, "Come on man, FB me" ("Facebook me," that is, use Facebook's encrypted application, WhatsApp) and "Don't call me; use Signal." It's not clear what consequences this has. Low-level dealers are easily replaced, and their disappearance from the street has little impact. Many in the law enforcement community have come to doubt that mandatory high sentencing for drug-related crimes leads to appreciable increases in public safety. Thus encryption and secured phones may not affect law enforcement's ultimate goal: keeping people safe.[39]

Meanwhile, communications metadata can reveal details of drug deals even when criminals work to cover their tracks. In 2008, Drug Enforcement Administration investigators found $900,000 in a tractor-trailer truck after a traffic stop in Detroit. The Mexican-based cartel had cleverly hidden their communication tracks by switching cellphones. This prevented law enforcement from obtaining wiretap orders, which require specificity on who is being tapped. Investigators instead used telephone billing records, cell tower information, and pen registers (which record all numbers dialed from a particular line) to find the Detroit-based criminals of the organization.[40]

When the easy solutions and work-arounds to encryption and anonymization don't work, law enforcement can do what the criminals do—hack in. As we know, the NSA breaks into systems (that's what signals-intelligence agencies do). The FBI has been conducting computer break-ins—searches—for over a decade. The technique is often used in child porn cases.[41]

The first known FBI computer intrusion, in 1999, involved a black-bag job, a key logger, and a mobster. Nicodemo Scarfo, Jr., appeared to be running a gambling and loan-sharking operation, but the files on his computer were encrypted and law-enforcement agents couldn't access them. The FBI broke in when Scarfo wasn't home, installing a device on his computer that would report his keystrokes. That device captured the cryptographic key that unlocked the files of his illegal activities. Like all such computer searches, this was done under court order.[42]

Although the key logger—the FBI's own design—worked well enough in this case, the bureau needed a better way to conduct wiretaps. Having to physically break into a racketeer's home to install a key logger is an activity best avoided. In 2007 the public learned of another computer intrusion. Someone with a MySpace address was emailing bomb threats to a Washington (State) high school. The messages were being funneled through a computer in Italy, making the perpetrator somewhat difficult to trace.[43]

An FBI agent impersonated a journalist and contacted the suspect, at one point emailing him links to photos with malware tucked inside. When the suspect opened the photos, his computer downloaded the software. The computer malware was fairly innocuous; it didn't harm the suspect's computer, search it, or steal. It simply provided the FBI server with the computer's information—its IP address, MAC address (a unique identifier assigned to a computer's network interface), current logged-on user name, running programs, and related information—and then the IP address and time and date of each subsequent connection. This was the computer's way of saying to the FBI, "I'm connecting, and here's where I live." The IP address told the FBI who provided the Internet connection (ISP); the date and time let them ask the ISP which customer had been connected at that time; and the MAC address, logged-on user name, and list of programs running identified which computer in the house was sending the threats. The FBI's spear-phishing approach worked, netting a high school student using his parents' computer to send the threats.[44]

In each of these cases, law enforcement agencies were

conducting "lawful hacking": lawful because the wiretap was installed under court order, and hacking because that's the technical means through which the tap is installed. The hacking itself was identical to the process by which criminals and other attackers use malware to extract data—but with a crucial difference. Law enforcement agencies obtain warrants before they hack. Hackers skip this step. Although the law is unclear on whether two search warrants—one for conducting the initial probe of the device, and the second for installing the wiretap—are necessary, that's the safer bet for law enforcement.[45]

Just like criminal hackers, lawful hackers generally operate through a two-step process. First, they probe the suspect's computer or smartphone to find out what systems it's running. Once law enforcement knows what's there, they're in a position to plant malware on the device or, in other words, hack it. Taking advantage of a vulnerability on the device—whether in the operating system or in an application—they install a wiretap. The wiretap may leak particular files, particular communications from the device (for instance, all emails, or all emails to a given party), or it may leak something a good deal smaller: the encryption key. If the key is leaked, wiretapping is really simple. All law enforcement has to do is collect the communication, and the encryption doesn't matter; law enforcement has the key. And any phone with a battery can be surreptitiously turned on, the microphone activated. All it takes is some rogue software on the user's phone, and it can be transformed into a listening device *without the user's knowledge*. In fact, intelligence and law enforcement agencies have been doing exactly this for at least a decade.[46]

The FBI typically deployed its tool for identifying the IP addresses of target machines within twenty-four to forty-eight hours of receiving a warrant. The bureau also developed or bought other tools for conducting remote computer surveillance. One of these, called "Magic Lantern," could wiretap as well as report communications metadata. And the FBI developed malware that could be delivered through a web browser when a user visited a targeted page (this is known as a "watering hole" attack).[47]

This last approach came in handy in Operation Torpedo, an FBI investigation directed against child porn sites. Dutch police had been investigating the Darknet—sites that aren't indexed on search engines and that are reachable only in a way that obscures the sites' IP addresses—when they got lucky: they found a misconfiguration error, that is, an administrative account left open without a password. This account, in turn, led them to a child porn site with an IP address belonging to an ISP in Bellevue, Nebraska. The Dutch investigators informed the FBI, which discovered that, unbeknownst to the ISP, an employee had given himself an account on which he was hosting the illicit material. Instead of immediately shutting down the site, however, the FBI decided to briefly run it—a controversial decision—in order to track the site's users.[48]

Site visitors used Tor to hide their tracks, which they believed made it impossible for the website to determine their IP addresses. But in Operation Torpedo, the FBI installed a NIT—a network investigative technique—that removed their anonymity. The NIT was a so-called drive-by download that installed itself on visitors' machines. Once there, the program reported the visitor's IP address, date and time of connection, machine OS (operating system), version, and architecture back to an FBI server. The FBI had netted not only the website's administrator, but also its users.[49]

In the cases I've discussed so far, the FBI used relatively simple technical methods to uncover who had been making bomb threats or downloading child porn. More capable criminals—a terrorist or a member of a sophisticated criminal organization, such as some of the drug cartels—often practice much better "operations security." But even sophisticated criminals struggle to keep this up over the long haul. A few small errors can be their undoing.

Consider the case of Silk Road, an online drug bazaar that also used Tor hidden services. Silk Road sold everything from cocaine to prescription medications. It was smooth and professional, with product description and service reviews that had the flash and professionalism of Amazon and eBay. Silk Road also appeared to have professional and savvy administrators. Funds were paid in Bitcoin and escrowed until the sale was complete. The site administrator, one "Dread Pirate Roberts," took a cut of each transaction, but had no contact with the drugs. These were sent via post (drug-sniffing dogs helped bring Silk Road to the attention of the DEA). Everything was carefully run—and difficult for law enforcement to break into.

Law enforcement agents started by arresting some participants. In some cases, they took over the suspects' accounts. There is some dispute over what happened next. In the official version of events, using a mistake in how the system had been set up, investigators were able to circumvent Tor and identify Silk Road's IP address. The site used CAPTCHAs—the annoying sets of letters and numbers users must type in to prove they are human—on its login page. Roberts's CAPTCHAs were from a CAPTCHA service. In a court deposition, an FBI agent said the CAPTCHAs leaked Silk Road's IP address.[50]

There are problems with this version of events. Various technologists say that the communications between the CAPTCHA server, a hidden site, and a user don't act in the ways the FBI described. The FBI agent's notes were lacking details on how this information was collected—an extreme oddity for forensic work—and the dates on the evidence show information being collected before the request had been placed. A more likely explanation is that an intelligence agency was monitoring connections to Iceland, found Silk Road's IP address, and tipped off the FBI.[51]

But even knowledge of the IP address wouldn't tell law enforcement where Roberts was, only where Silk Road was hosted: Reykjavik. Armed with this legal documentation, US law enforcement officials flew to Iceland. They returned with a hard drive that mirrored Silk Road's server. Silk Road appeared to be grossing $600 million annually. By now, the FBI, DHS, DEA, and the Internal Revenue Service (IRS) had all become involved in the investigation.[52]

An FBI investigator started studying the computer connections supporting the business. Information from the copied server cast light on tantalizing clues strewn across the Internet. An IRS investigator found that a user with the screen name "Altoid" had promoted Silk Road on a website devoted to "magic" mushrooms. When the investigator Googled "Altoid," he discovered that a user using that name in an Internet chat room had asked about configuring Tor hidden services around the time that Silk Road was being set up. The user said replies should go to rossulbricht@gmail.com, then changed his screen name to "Frosty." The hard drive showed one trusted computer was allowed to log in to all Silk Road servers, using encryption keys that ended in "frosty@frosty."[53]

A search of government federal databases turned up a DHS report on one Ross Ulbricht, who possessed multiple faked IDs. His last known address was a short distance from a San Francisco Internet café whose IP address matched that of an administrator's login to Silk Road. With this information, the FBI obtained the appropriate search warrants. From there, the only thing left was to make sure that Ulbricht's laptop was open—and therefore unencrypted—when he was arrested. The FBI nabbed Ulbricht at the Glen Park Branch Library in San Francisco, where he was logged on. Two undercover cops created a disturbance just behind him. While Ulbricht turned to look, the undercover agent across from him grabbed his open laptop, using an extremely low-tech, yet effective, trick to bypass encryption.[54]

Improved patching and system security have conspired to make lawful hacking more difficult. The FBI can't rely on poorly configured and unpatched systems as a way in to wiretap. Nor can it count on distracting criminals who happen to have their laptops open. If the FBI wants content, and not just metadata, it has to develop more sophisticated ways to access targeted devices.

This means using zero-day vulnerabilities, ones that are not yet publicly known or patched. Zero days are hard to find (that's what made Stuxnet's use of five different zero days so extraordinary) and expensive to buy. A government investigator seeking to hack in can expect to pay anywhere from a few thousand dollars to seven figures for a zero-day vulnerability. The price depends on the prevalence of the underlying platform—a vulnerability against the Chrome browser is worth much more than one against Safari, for example—and other factors, like whether the buyer is demanding exclusive use.

Using zero days to hack into criminals' encrypted systems puts the government smack in the middle of a security and ethical conflict. If investigators report the zero day to the manufacturer, they lose the potential for using it later. If they don't, they risk that someone else, hackers working for criminal organizations or other nations, may find and exploit it against their own citizens. In a report issued in 2017, RAND Corporation researchers observed that the time from finding a zero day to exploiting it is typically short (a median of twenty-two days), that most exploits have a long average life expectancy (6.9 years), and that few researchers find the same vulnerabilities. This, at least, argues against the need for immediate reporting.[55]

But what if the vulnerability is against a widely used system, or one that controls important infrastructure? Surely immediate reporting is crucial in such cases. Indeed, the US Department of Defense's "Vulnerabilities Equity Policy" implies that is US policy. Reports in early 2017 that the CIA had been stockpiling unreported capabilities against commonly used systems—such as Android and iPhones—suggests that the government has not yet found the appropriate balance.[56]

Criminals are getting smarter, and, with or without the help of Silicon Valley, they are employing ever-better security protections. Lawful hacking is a technically—and morally—complex investigative solution, but law enforcement doesn't really have a choice. Security has always been a cat-and-mouse game; if you position more guards at the bank's door, the criminals will blast into the vault through the basement. Law enforcement agencies must develop ways to handle encrypted communications and secured devices.[57]

The FBI can also rely on outside help. When the law enforcement agency bought its way into the San Bernardino terrorist's phone, it illuminated a clandestine market of data-forensics tools. An Israeli company, Cellebrite, a major supplier of data-extraction tools for law enforcement around the world, was rumored to be the source of the Apple hack.[58]

Cellebrite started off as a company enabling data extraction to move users' contact lists and the like from an old phone to a new one. When digital forensics became important to law enforcement, Cellibrite moved into that market. The company derives its capabilities from a combination of close relationships with phone manufacturers, who let Cellebrite learn a phone's design months before the device hits the market, and highly talented technologists, who "reverse engineer" the system to determine exactly how security features work. But Cellebrite also relies on less arcane methods: some of its tools appear quite similar to iOS "jail breaking" tools available over the Internet.[59]

Cellebrite builds devices to extract call logs, contacts, calendars, SMS (texts), media files, apps data, chats, and passwords off locked phones—though not for every type of phone, of course. The company's technology can even resurrect deleted SMS messages and call histories from the phone's flash memory chip.[60]

Cellebrite's devices, like the tools of its competitors, are plug-and-play. They have many different capabilities. Simple data-transfer systems are sold to phone stores, which move their customers' data from old phones to new ones. Devices that can extract data from locked phones are also sold to universities to train forensic investigators. Their training courses cover topics from the elementary—how to handle evidence and how data extraction works—to the complex. "Smartphone extraction," for instance, shows how to safely remove and copy a device's memory chip to get around the encryption and extract the secured data. Tools like this are a boon for police forces, especially for departments that aren't in a position to field a technology unit.[61]

With so many new, rich sources of data available, with hacking tools for sale, and with access to at least some in-house expertise and specialized contractors, why does law enforcement claim to be going dark? Why aren't agencies taking advantage of these capabilities? The short answer is: they are. The longer response is: it's complicated.

First, and most obviously, these new data-analysis tools are expensive. Their price tags often surpass what small- and medium-sized cities can pay. And yet, state and local police conduct two-thirds of wiretaps and most phone searches.

A second problem is unfamiliarity with the forensic technology itself. Too often, law enforcement investigators aren't entirely clear on what, exactly, they're attempting to hack, producing a situation computer scientists call "GIGO": garbage in, garbage out. Jonathan Zdziarski is an Apple forensics expert whom the US Army hired to examine phone evidence in the case of a brigadier general accused of sexual harassment, assault, and making murder threats. Zdziarski examined whether evidence on the phone had been added or deleted; he discovered that the forensic tools initially used in the investigation were badly flawed. The tools made up access times because the operating system lacked that data, listed an app as deleted based on the next time the device booted up—and not when the app was actually deleted—and miscalculated the date when an app was used. After Zdziarski's analysis, the most serious accusations against the brigadier general were dismissed.[62]

A third problem, one that FBI general counsel Caproni alluded to, is that investigations in the digital era are increasingly complex. A case might involve evidence in the form of emails, phone calls, and instant messages, each of which may go through a different provider. In the process of investigating a single suspect, a detective might need access to information from a half-dozen providers—Verizon for a suspect's smartphone account, Apple for iMessage data, AT&T for a landline account, Google for personal email, Sonic.net for home ISP, Comcast for work ISP. Even the process of obtaining the communications metadata, intended to be simple, can be daunting for a state or local investigator. Law enforcement officials frequently find themselves requesting information from providers who are accessible only via a web form, not a person. *CSI* it's not.

A fourth problem is that, unlike crimes committed in the past, an offense and its instigator are often thousands of miles apart. In a financial fraud case, credit card information might be lifted from a store in Miami, shipped to Ukraine, and then used by a criminal in New York. Local law enforcement is not equipped to handle such investigations.[63]

Neither is the legal system. As with the Silk Road case, there are systems in place for nations to provide legal assistance for obtaining evidence in a criminal investigation. These mutual legal assistance treaties, put in place during a different era, don't work at Internet speed—even though the criminals do. This is a problem that badly needs fixing.

What do state and local law enforcement do now when their digital investigations involve other countries? One state investigator told me that local law enforcement often decides to ignore reported thefts of small amounts—say, a few hundred dollars. They focus instead on local crimes they can solve; often, that's child pornography investigations. This response helps explain the otherwise baffling discrepancy between the seriousness of Internet fraud and the lack of interest in prosecuting it: in 2015 alone, the FBI reported an estimated $1 billion loss, but only nineteen convictions.[64]

When the FBI took Apple to court in February 2016, the law enforcement agency claimed that only Apple could write the necessary software to access the iPhone's data. Within weeks, however, one hacking company got the FBI into the phone— and charged the government $1 million for its effort. A few months later, a Cambridge University researcher showed how to hack the phone using chip-mirroring techniques. His total cost was about $100, spent on purchasing supplies on eBay. Cellebrite also claimed to be able to get in. Apparently, there were more ways into the iPhone than the FBI had imagined. The FBI looked for a legal workaround when what it really needed was a technological solution.[65]

Technology seems to stump many law enforcement investigators. Zdziarski, the iPhone forensics expert, observed that in the early days of smartphones, FBI technologists were eager to understand the technology. But as automatic tools for analyzing data became available, the bureau put less emphasis on developing its own expertise. Agents wanted "push-and-drool" solutions: press a button, get the data. This turned out to be the wrong answer. Cellebrite and similar tools are fine, but investigators need to fully understand the tools' limitations—as Zdziarski did in the investigation of the brigadier general. More to the point, law enforcement needs the ability to either develop its own solutions or supervise its consultants when current tools, whether homegrown or purchased, can't produce the desired information.[66]

The FBI undoubtedly has some very good technical people—it just doesn't have enough of them. The 2017 budget request for developing tools for countering encryption and anonymization—it's called the "Going Dark" program—is only $70 million and thirty-nine people. That's woefully inadequate for the scale of the problem. The complexity of our new communications technologies requires law enforcement to develop commensurate technological expertise.[67]

Investigators need to know, for example, how phones work. How do you pull information off a particular phone? What's all the information that can be removed from the phone? Where is it stored? Are there copies of deleted information? What data from the phone may be in the cloud, instead of on the phone itself? How is data about an app determined? Does the date in the log refer to the last time the app was used, the last time it was accessed, or the last time the operating system was rebooted?

Investigators need to understand how communications protocols work. In 2015 the Manhattan district attorney's office noted that information about Apple's iMessages was not at the telecommunications carriers—the normal place for such metadata. It's hard to know why they made the statement; one implication might be that the data should be at the carriers. Was this an opening salvo for a new law on what information the companies should store? In fact, the data—the to/from information of iMessages—was stored on Apple servers, and the Manhattan investigators should have known that. They should know similar information about other communications protocols. WhatsApp messages are end-to-end encrypted, but are there circumstances where messages might be in the clear? These are the kinds of issues that investigators must understand.[68]

For law enforcement and prosecutors to do their jobs effectively, many more investigators will need to learn the nitty-gritty details of how contemporary communication technologies work. These details change quickly; investigators have to stay up to date—and yet also be comprehensive. In many cases, criminals do not use the most sophisticated technology, and inexpensive, older methods of accessing data will suffice. Other times, they will not, but law enforcement may be able to glean sufficient information from other sources. To do its job effectively, the criminal justice system needs to have access to people with the deep technical skills to handle encrypted communications and locked phones. Only then will law enforcement be in a position to make reasoned judgments about which cases warrant expending resources on—and which cases do not.

State and local investigators are not completely on their own. There are all sorts of short courses: the Secret Service's National Computer Forensics Institute teaches how to recover data from devices, while the National White Collar Crime Center, a nonprofit, shows the fundamentals of high-tech crime investigations: getting and analyzing call records, best practices for seizing a phone (phones need to be put into a "Faraday cage," which shields the phone from radio waves and prevents the phone from being remotely wiped—aluminum foil will do nicely), examining phones, monitoring and capturing Internet traffic. Basic stuff, but critical for investigators.[69]

Not to be left out, the FBI has the National Domestic Communications Assistance Center (NDCAC), which also provides training and some consultation on how modern communications technologies, devices, and services work. It, too, does the basic stuff. "A lot of the solutions are less about the intercept [wiretap]," one member of law enforcement told me, "than about making sense of what the provider gives you." Want to know the legal process for acquiring a particular type of communications data? How long till a particular provider deletes the data? What tools are available to access various types of devices? NDCAC's hotline is open from 6 a.m. to midnight Monday to Friday—with email response 24/7.[70]

Despite calls for this type of solution a half dozen years ago, NDCAC only got off the ground in 2015. While its creation is a step in the right direction, as of this writing, the center does not address the types of sophisticated cyberattack and cyberexploit problems that the nation faces. Nor does NDCAC conduct its own research on pressing issues like opening phones or determining how to successfully wiretap when encryption is in the way.[71]

The FBI faces real challenges in developing the depth of technical expertise it needs. In theory, it is not impossible to attract really smart hackers and technologists to government work. The NSA, for example, has been quite successful in making these hires, despite the higher salaries of Silicon Valley. The FBI is a different type of agency than the storied NSA, more of a crime-fighting bureau that esteems the physically fit agent who races after the bad guy on foot, not via bits. But bad guys are bad guys, even if their handiwork is in bits. If the FBI tries hard enough to recruit them, some hackers will surely be attracted to the challenge.

The Secret Service has already figured one small way to do this. This law enforcement agency doesn't just protect the president; it also hacks phones—not for tracking terrorists, but for protecting the US financial system, another Secret Service responsibility. The Secret Service set up a tiny phone-cracking unit at the University of Tulsa in 2008. With two agents, some faculty, and college students enrolled in a government cybersecurity scholarship program, the center cracks forty phones a year. But its real purpose is training the students, whose scholarships require that they work for the government after they graduate. They use Cellebrite, but also develop their own methods for opening up and extracting data from the less commonly used phones (these are the ones for which Cellebrite doesn't work). The devices come from state and local police departments that need help with the password-protected phones.[72]

The experience of the Manhattan Attorney's Office shows that it is, in fact, possible to make law enforcement agencies attractive places for people with this kind of expertise. Under Cy Vance, the office has created a cyber investigations lab filled with lawyers and techies working together, seventy-five people in all. With a quarter of the city's cases involving digital evidence, the lab does forensics, tracks criminals through their cellular locations (and simultaneously recognizes the limitations of this information), handles credit card theft—and more. Three Russian speakers on staff troll the dark corners of the web where criminals gather, investigating Internet fraud. New York, at least, is meeting twenty-first-century crimes with twenty-first-century solutions.[73]

As the Russian attacks on the 2016 US presidential campaign demonstrated, the Digital Revolution radically changed what our assets are and how those assets can be stolen or attacked. Understanding these changes and responding to them appropriately is very much the responsibility of the FBI director. That the director responded to the San Bernardino case by asking for the removal of Apple's "guard dogs"—the phone's security protections—shows that, even as the world around him had changed, the director continued to see investigations through twentieth-century techniques.[74]

Networking and digitization have empowered our twenty-first-century enemies—organized crime and nation-state attackers—enabling them to steal and attack at scale and from a distance. Individuals, corporations, and security agencies use twenty-first-century technologies, including end-to-end encryption and secured devices, to protect their data and systems. That means that law enforcement must develop twenty-first-century capabilities for conducting investigations. Law enforcement should be pursuing these paths forward with alacrity.[75]

6

There's No Turning Back

I like to start my day with a paper copy of the *New York Times*. Over a cup of tea, I begin with the front page's rightmost column and work my way through the first section. Though reading online has its benefits—up-to-the-moment news and availability, whether I'm in San Francisco, Seoul, or Spoleto—when I read online I tend to look at lighter stories. So I prefer starting my day with the paper copy. But it's becoming harder for travelers and people who don't subscribe to find one. In 1993, the *Times*'s daily circulation was 1.2 million papers; in 2016, circulation had nearly doubled, but the number of paper copies had dropped in half. The result? Outside New York City, it can be difficult to find a paper copy of the *Times*.[1]

Blame it on the Digital Revolution. The convenience of online reading and instant updates trumped the pleasures of reading on paper. The *Times* even dropped its large-print edition because the ease of increasing print size on tablets removed the need for that version.

There's no returning to print newspapers, offices filled with secretaries typing, or factories brimming with people assembling small devices or large machines. Networking and bits control the factory floor, critical infrastructure, medical devices—even the harvesting of crops. Network connectivity has undoubtedly created many efficiencies, but it has also fundamentally changed the nature of security risks. Beginning in the mid-1980s, we saw the start of cyberexploits and cyberattacks. At first these were against military sites, but when Internet commerce started, the information available—and the attacks—vastly expanded. The threat picked up speed in the 2000s and 2010s. All sectors—industry, healthcare, the government, even private individuals—were under attack.

The US criminal justice system, in the meantime, was finding that new modes of communications were making it hard to wiretap. Law enforcement wanted access to encrypted communications. The FBI's push for this access was gaining momentum when the 2013 Snowden disclosures on NSA surveillance stopped the FBI's efforts in its tracks.

At that point, the public discussion on surveillance shifted heavily toward protecting privacy, and Internet companies began to make encryption the default setting, not just for communications, but also for securing phones. In the decade since the iPhone was introduced, text-messaging apps have overtaken phone calls as the most popular way to communicate (calls are a close second), and phones have become the most popular way of accessing the Internet. The phones have also become repositories for personal information: contacts, texts, photos, health information, and the like. Individuals and companies quite reasonably want to keep the information stored on these phones secure and private.[2]

After the terrorist attacks in Paris, San Bernardino, and elsewhere, however, the pendulum began to shift back away from privacy. Intelligence and law enforcement agencies, most notably the General Communications Headquarters, Britain's equivalent of the NSA, and the FBI began pressing to control encryption's use. They spoke of a "golden key" or "exceptional access" that would let investigators with legal authority read communications despite strong encryption.

In the summer and fall of 2016, the United States finally experienced an unstabilizing attack. I am speaking, of course, of the Russian cyberexploit against the Democratic National Committee (DNC), the email theft that may have changed the outcome of the 2016 US presidential election. The attack and its repercussions overturned all previous calculations about cybersecurity. The real surprise is that we didn't see the attack coming.

The United States and other nations, including Australia, Canada, and the United Kingdom, practiced for an attack. They conducted cyberwar gaming exercises in which they tested responses to jammed GPS, destructive cyberattacks against critical infrastructure, and DDoS attacks against banks and businesses. These war games revealed strains in coordinating responses from civilian and military agencies and multiple allies—all of which would be necessary in a real cyberattack. In response, the governments improved their capabilities. And yet: the United States was not prepared.[3]

The exploit itself—the theft of emails and documents from the Democratic National Committee and the Democratic Congressional Campaign Committee—was not unusual; the technique to break in—spear phishing—unsurprising. The uncommon aspect of the attack was the use to which the theft was put: during the last weeks of a presidential campaign, Wiki-Leaks made the emails public. American democratic institutions —the government, political parties, and civic infrastructure—

were taken by surprise. It is not remotely clear how to prevent the next such attack by a canny and merciless enemy.

The Digital Revolution simplified Russia's ability to conduct psychological warfare abroad. Private Russian citizens, not the Russian state, carried out the DDoS attacks on Estonia and Georgia in 2007 and 2008, respectively. But actions by the government at the time made clear that it condoned the activity and would protect the perpetrators. Similarly, the 2015 attacks on the Ukrainian power grid had no official connection to the Russian government, even though it was clear they came from Russia and had been given a green light by the government. Russian leadership was certainly willing to use cyber to sow chaos when it saw political or military value in doing so.[4]

In 2016, Moscow used its new technique to disrupt events abroad. Russian security forces are old hands at smearing opponents with faked photos, fake stories, and propaganda. It was a standard tool of governance during the Soviet era.

All governments seek to encourage support and tilt press releases (negative stories, such as an increase in unemployment, are often announced on Friday afternoons for minimal coverage). But the Soviet Union took this effort to a new, and rather extraordinary, level. In creating the new Soviet man, the Soviet Communist Party envisioned an energetic individual who would propel the revolution, whether in breaking records through laying bricks or in Olympic gymnastics. Central to this story was the government's control of all forms of public discourse: newspapers, radio, and, then later, television broadcasts and public meetings. Though the name of the official party newspaper, *Pravda,* meant truth, the news in it was anything but. Citizens of the Soviet satellite states—Czechoslovakia, East

Germany, Hungary, Poland, and Romania—whose governments were essentially controlled by the Soviet Union, faced the same manipulation of facts.[5]

In retrospect, the Russian approach to the US presidential election seems obvious. Don't bother tampering with the ballot box, which could affect the legitimacy of the election. Instead, tamper with what the public hears. Americans would accept the vote's outcome despite having been manipulated.

That's what happened. US intelligence agencies—the CIA, FBI, and NSA—concluded that Russian intelligence conducted cyberexploits against US political parties with deliberate intent to "undermine public faith in the US democratic process, denigrate Secretary Clinton, and harm her electability and potential presidency." Extraordinary. Regardless of how one feels about the outcome of the election—or the fact that the United States has previously meddled in other nations' elections—no one now doubts that our dependence on cyber presents an extremely serious threat to the United States, and that Russia is the nation most prepared to use it.[6]

In 2015, the nominee for chair of the Joint Chiefs of Staff, Marine general Joe Dunford, said, "Russia presents the greatest threat to our national security." Six months later, Director of National Intelligence James Clapper described cyberthreats as the United States' biggest threat. They were both right. As Clapper testified after the attacks, "Russia is a full-scope cyber actor that poses a major threat to US government, military, diplomatic, commercial, and critical infrastructure and key resource networks."[7]

Nor is the United States the only nation in Russian gunsights. TV5Monde, a twelve-channel network that is France's answer to the BBC, very nearly disappeared in April 2015. For three hours, the network was off the air, the victim of a cyberattack that corrupted Internet-connected hardware controlling the station's operations. During the outage, TV5Monde's Facebook page posted the "identity cards and CVs of relatives of French soldiers involved in anti-ISIS operations." A group supposedly linked to ISIS, calling itself the "Cyber Caliphate," claimed responsibility for the attack. But it turns out there was no Cyber Caliphate—only Russian hackers.[8]

Like the attack against the three Ukrainian power distribution systems, the attack against TV5Monde was carefully researched, with extensive reconnaissance. The hackers tailored their attack to work against TV5Monde's system. And in fact, the attack would have been worse had the timing been slightly different—the network had just launched another channel, so technicians were on hand. One quick-thinking technician disconnected the corrupted machine from the Internet, saving the rest of the system. This sophisticated effort was most likely a rehearsal for a larger attack against a different target.[9]

Using the same playbook that had worked in the United States, the Russians tried to disrupt the 2017 French presidential election. They ran false news stories that claimed candidate François Fillon had recovered in the polls, and published stolen internal communications of the leading candidate, Emmanuel Macron, in the final days of the campaign. Macron won nonetheless.[10]

To the West, Russian-sponsored cyberattacks were unexpectedly hostile actions during a time of peaceful, though cold, relations. But to Russia, they were a deserved response to what the country's leadership saw as a quarter-century of Western aggression against Russian sovereignty.[11]

Understanding this situation requires a brief foray into post–Cold War history. When the Soviet Union dissolved in 1991, many nations on its periphery became independent.

Western nations immediately stepped in, providing aid of various sorts, in hopes of moving these states toward democratic institutions and alliances with the West. Media networks, including CNN and the BBC, sent reporters abroad; nongovernmental organizations (NGOs) invested in developing the institutions of civil society; and new communication technologies simplified the task of building political organizations. The former Soviet republics in the Baltic and the Eastern European satellites became democracies; most eventually joined the European Union and NATO.

Western leaders described what was happening as a healthy and natural transition. Russian leaders saw the situation entirely differently—and with great anger. Instead of fostering democracy, the creation of a free press and civil society organizations was a way to stir dissent and create regime change. To Russians, this was an attack—an attack without guns and tanks, but an attack nonetheless.

The Balkan wars (1991–2001) provided another source of conflict. The death of Yugoslav leader Josip Tito in 1980 presaged the nation's breakup a decade later. The violent civil war that resulted included a campaign of "ethnic cleansing" conduced by Bosnian Serbs against Bosnian Muslims and Croatians. In 1999 NATO conducted air strikes to halt the Serbian actions. From the perspective of Washington and the Western European capitals, the NATO intervention prevented a full-scale genocide. In Moscow's eyes, the NATO bombings were illegal, as they hadn't been approved by the UN Security Council. (Russia, of course, would have vetoed any resolution approving NATO intervention.)

Revolutions—the "Velvet" revolution in Czechoslovakia (1989); the "Rose" revolution in Georgia (2003); the "Orange" revolution in Ukraine (2004); the Arab Spring (2010–2012) in

countries across North Africa and the Arabian Peninsula—
blossomed during this period. Once again, the West saw these
events as democratic uprisings against repressive regimes (some
more successful than others), while Russia saw a more sinister
plot: a Western iron hand, cloaked in a velvet glove. Russia
found the changes destabilizing. The government worried that
such revolutions could threaten even the Russian regime itself.[12]

Where the Western leaders saw tools such as economic
sanctions as a way to apply political pressure and avoid more
aggressive military responses against Russian aggression in
Crimea and eastern Ukraine, Moscow considered such actions
"nonmilitary measures of war." Moscow interpreted these nonmilitary responses as literally war by other means.[13]

In the early 2010s, Moscow decided it had had enough of
Western interference in its affairs, enough of Western war by
other means. In 2013 Russia's chief of general staff, Gen. Valery
Gerasimov, laid out the new strategy. Russia would blur the
line between war and peace, "fighting a war without fighting
a war," in the words of US Marine general Robert Neller, who
studied Gerasimov's strategy. There'd be no blitzkrieg, no Operation Desert Storm with heavy bombing. Russia's response
would be subtle, hidden, difficult to attribute, and it would be
full of, as Neller put it, "disinformation, deception; the use of
special forces to engage with local forces that may have a political beef with their own country."[14]

What better tool to accomplish this than cyber? By the
2010s, the West had grown heavily dependent on networked
systems, most of which remained poorly secured. At the same
time, Russia had a cadre of highly skilled hackers, many of
whom had honed their capabilities in criminal activity. The
government began hiring hackers in great numbers, and the
Russian government's undercover war took off.[15]

Russia had a great advantage in this asymmetric battle. Its campaign involved hostile actions in the midst of peace, attacks without dead bodies (or many of them), and disruption that was expensive but didn't rise to the cost of a few lost fighter jets (a single F-15 costs $100 million). Yet retaliating in kind would have been impossible, even if the will were there. Russia is not as wired as some of the nations it sought to attack, limiting the potential for damage. And US military doctrine does not permit deliberately targeting civilian artifacts.[16]

The potential damage to democratic societies from an avalanche of propaganda, leaks, and damage through cyber-exploits and the like is extremely high. In both Georgia and Ukraine, for example, such attacks created fear and uncertainty. According to US Director of National Intelligence Clapper, "In foreign countries, Russian actors conducted damaging and/or disruptive cyberattacks. . . . In some cases Russian intelligence actors have masqueraded as third parties, hiding behind false online personas designed to cause the victim to misattribute the source of the attack. . . . Russia has also used cyber tactics and techniques to seek to influence public opinion across Europe and Eurasia." Or as the *Guardian* put it, "Watch out, Europe. Germany is top of Russian hackers' list."[17]

The implications for modern states are chilling. In the case of the DNC attack, the hackers used the fruits of cyber-exploits to influence the election for president. Imagine something worse. What if, instead of stealing information, adversaries compromise information in US computer systems? What if the information being corrupted were bank account information, done over a period of time so that backups were also corrupted? Or the data recorded for determining the efficacy of a new drug? Or the instructions used by a million-dollar assembly-line robot? Factory antics in real life are not nearly as humorous as the ones depicted in Charlie Chaplin's classic film *Modern Times*. They can, in fact, be quite destructive. If you're intent on creating mischief and disrupting a state, industrialized nations offer a greatly rising number of targets. Many use poor authentication procedures, thus increasing risk—not decreasing it.[18]

For decades, military strategists had worried about the possibility of a devastating cyberattack. But in recent years, this talk receded, as policy strategists realized that the interconnections between nations' economies—the fact, for instance, that the Chinese government had a big investment in US government bonds—limited the interest of those nations most capable of conducting such an attack from actually doing so. (This reasoning doesn't apply, of course, when economies are disconnected, as is the case for the United States and North Korea.) The Russian cyberattack—and though the action was an information theft, the word "attack" is accurate in this context—showed that civil society's infrastructure—the press, think tanks, universities—was the soft spot.

In the innocent times before the DNC hack, government and private-sector analysts characterized cybersecurity threats primarily as the theft of military, government, and industry secrets—all of which grew increasingly serious in the 2000s and 2010s. Then in 2015 the United States and China agreed to outlaw cyberespionage for commercial gain. China signed a similar agreement with the United Kingdom a month later, and then with Russia, Brazil, and the Group of Twenty (nineteen major countries plus the EU) in November 2015.[19]

The US-China agreement doesn't outlaw spying for military purposes—the United States would never have signed if it had. Commentators expressed significant cynicism about the agreement. But to virtually everyone's surprise, intellectual property (IP) theft from China, already dropping in 2015, sharply decreased after the agreement was formalized. Opinions vary as to why; some have speculated that the drop had more to do with Chinese President Xi Jinping's attempts to crack down on Internet use than with diplomatic agreements. The importance of publicity about China's hacking, including US indictments of five Chinese hackers and threats of possible economic sanctions, cannot be discounted. Chinese authorities didn't like the public embarrassment stemming from the charges. But whatever the reasons, Chinese cyberexploits have decreased since the signing of this agreement.[20]

Security experts had also been warning for years about the threats cyberattacks posed to critical infrastructure. Here the situation is not entirely bleak. Some critical infrastructure sectors—banking is one case—have implemented better security measures. Even if the changes should have happened ten (or more) years ago, better late than never.

The attacks on the DNC and on the Ukrainian power distribution companies—which could have been much worse had the attackers wanted to make them so—show an enemy intent on creating disruption. Imagine: what if someone launched simultaneous attacks against the press during the final days before an election? Or caused power failures on the US East Coast just after a Category 5 hurricane hit Florida? Many bad things are possible when there's a determined and technically capable adversary.

Critical infrastructure has weaknesses in the industrial control systems that control power grids, oil and natural gas pipelines, and machinery on the factory floor. Improvement is definitely possible. Industrial control systems are simple—think 1980s-style PCs, not modern computers—and not subject to the constant churn of IT systems. Currently the systems are vulnerable because vendors and owners don't think strong security is worth the cost. But determination, money—and government regulation—could change that. Best to do so before Moscow's long-distance cybergames include manipulating the pressure on a pipeline, causing it to explode. Russia is believed to be responsible for just such an attack against a Turkish oil pipeline in 2008.[21]

The really unsettling aspect of the Russian cyberattacks is the extent of what needs securing; it's not just—just?—the government, the military, and business anymore. In any government that's "of the people, by the people, for the people," the sine qua non for trust in government is that important decisions or developments have ample room for public discussion and debate. Democracies rely on the press to keep people informed. We know that the Russian government spies on journalists, tapping their phones, reading their emails. That includes emails in protected US accounts; the Yahoo mail account of Anna Politkovskaya, a Russian investigative journalist, was hacked a year before she was murdered (it is unknown who ordered her death, but it is presumed to have been the Russian government).[22]

And then there's civil society. Political scientists observe that a vigorous civil society leads to a more responsive government. Civic organizations—from avowedly political ones to groups that only occasionally participate in politics—channel the public's voices to the debate. US intelligence agencies reported that think tanks and lobbying groups "viewed as likely to shape future US policies" were also targets of Russian hacking during the 2016 election. That leaves dynamic democracies with literally millions of soft spots.[23]

The DNC has now, belatedly, secured its systems. Indeed,

the *Wall Street Journal* reported broad bipartisan use of encrypted communications after news of the DNC hack: "Political aides close to President Donald Trump, former President Barack Obama, and former Secretary of State Hillary Clinton are [all using Signal]." But it was too little, too late.[24]

The 2016 activity may be just the tip of the iceberg. This time, the hacking was data theft used to embarrass and mock a presidential candidate. Next time, the hacking might take the form of corrupted computer files—a journalist's notes, a think tank's public policy recommendations, a university professor's scientific data on climate change—effectively sowing falsehoods and creating a distrust of the press, civic organizations, and such authorities as think tanks, universities, and, ultimately, the government. The Russian government's tactics to delegitimize Western governments have been quite effective to date.

No one had anticipated that a technically capable enemy would attack the United States in this way. Regardless of how one feels about NSA surveillance, many layers of law and regulations constrain how the US government collects and uses national-security surveillance. The Russian government is not bound by a similar set of laws. Putin's Russia is a powerful, sophisticated, and ruthless government. It has conducted assassinations of businesspeople, journalists, and political activists—both within Russia's borders and beyond. It plays for keeps. The Western world—and the United States in particular—was unprepared for Russia's attacks against Western civil society.[25]

In testifying to Congress about risks posed by encryption, FBI director Comey spoke about the need for balancing the principles of public safety, national security, and privacy. From law enforcement's perspective, end-to-end encryption and locked devices pose problems for investigating terrorism, drug, and child-porn investigations. But the best public safety and security comes from careful and thoughtful analysis of what the most dangerous threats are, rather than which threats are most viscerally upsetting.[26]

On initial consideration, it might seem as if encryption without the possibility of exceptional access pits public safety, national security, and privacy against each other. Such a framing misses the fundamental changes in our lives brought about by the Digital Revolution: our reliance on networked systems and digital devices; our constant installing and updating of insecure apps; our blithe, casual approach to security, in which people seek another route to access if strong security gets in their way. The better way to understand the debate about encryption and locked devices is through the competing needs of law enforcement and society. Law enforcement wants access to evidence; society wants—and desperately needs—communications and data security.

Our greatest threat comes from Russia, described by no less an authority than former Director of National Intelligence James Clapper as an "existential threat" to the West. As we've seen from the attacks against the United States during the 2016 election—and similar efforts elsewhere--the Russian efforts are directed not just against the government, but also against civil society. And that means people participating in public life must be in a position to securely protect their data and communications.[27]

Strong encryption—meaning a strong algorithm with keys properly secured, and not compromised through back doors, front doors, or exceptional access—supports public safety, national security, and privacy. End-to-end encryption protects against eavesdroppers. Forward secrecy, which cannot be employed under exceptional-access requirements, prevents previous communications from being decrypted if the key is later discovered (a particularly useful feature against a nation-state threat). Secure phones provide a strong system for multifactor authentication, protecting against data and identity theft. None of these tools will fully solve the cyber-security problem, but they are essential for our security.

By securing communications and making authentication easy, end-to-end encryption and secured devices decrease the risk of crime and increase public safety. They make it more difficult for Russia and other nation-state attackers to break into systems, thus improving national security. End-to-end encryption and secured devices increase people's safety, which explains why so many people are now turning to secure messaging platforms. (Signal saw a 400 percent increase in daily downloads in the last months of 2016.) Protecting data through end-to-end encryption and secured devices increases privacy as well.[28]

After the Snowden disclosures, US tech companies lost customers. Cloud computing services, which provide shared computing resources, were particularly hard hit; various companies and countries wanted to locate their data centers outside the United States to make them less accessible to US intelligence. Despite the tensions, United States–based tech companies like Google and Facebook remained the repositories of large amounts of personal information from citizens around the world; this was in large part because consumers trust them. The US law enforcement and national security communities benefit; it gives them a home team advantage for getting at data under court order.[29]

Such trust by users is a fragile thing. If exceptional access were required, it would undermine the trust that people in other nations have in US tech companies. By making the United States a less attractive location in which to store data, policies that require exceptional access could make US law enforcement and national security agencies' job much more difficult—not less.

We've already seen that law enforcement has many tools available to it, even with end-to-end encryption and secured phones. The existence of evidence doesn't mean that law enforcement has a right to it. Former Department of Homeland Security secretary Michael Chertoff noted, "If you stand back and look historically, very often you couldn't get evidence because of other values." In the United States, courts reject evidence if its collection violated a warrant or was obtained without a needed warrant.[30]

The Digital Revolution and its accompanying "Golden Age of Surveillance" have given law enforcement access to more evidence than ever before. The plethora of sources—communications metadata, social media, information stored in the cloud, location data provided by cell towers and other sources (including highway and public transit toll-collection systems), automated license plate readers, video from surveillance cameras—has changed the nature of investigations. In many cases, investigators find that this information makes it much easier to figure out—and prove—the who, what, where of a crime. Undoubtedly, encryption has made it more difficult to collect some of this new evidence. But the protection encryption offers has also made it more difficult for organized crime and nation-states intent on stealing data, creating disruptions, and attacking systems to wreak havoc.

The prospect of attack by foreign agents is particularly alarming. It is not an exaggeration to say that attacks by foreign states against US civil society have the potential to severely destabilize democracy. Political espionage by opponents is an old game, but under the old rules, attackers, presumed to be domestic opponents, were constrained by the threat of capture and prosecution. Foreign attackers, enabled by the distance-leveling of networked systems, are able to operate with great impunity.[31]

The Russian attack on the DNC showed that organizations that didn't think of themselves as potential targets of cyberattacks—cyberespionage, yes; cyberattacks, no—most definitely are. Politicians have long understood that their private lives are at risk of exposure, but private citizens participating in civil society have not generally expected their private lives to become public fodder. The Russian attacks sharply change the equation for democratic participation.

The US government has debated the dangers to civil society of surveillance before, most notably in the 1970s, when the Senate's Church Committee investigated the intelligence agencies' spying on, among other things, domestic political organizations. On a number of occasions, this information was then used to discredit people opposing government policies. That's dangerous—and highly destabilizing—for a democracy. The committee's report observed that, where government surveillance occurs, "Persons most intimidated may well not be those at the extremes of the political spectrum, but rather those nearer the middle. Yet voices of moderation are vital to balance public debate and avoid polarization of our society." Citizen participation—marching in favor of women's rights or against abortion, or speaking for an increase in the minimum wage or a decrease in immigration quotas—is crucial for democratic societies. If participating in civil society puts people at risk of exposing their private lives—a father-in-law with drinking problems, a child with epilepsy, an affair—people pull back from involvement; they fall silent. The risk of public exposure creates a negative incentive for actively participating in civil society.[32]

The Church Committee's report addressed how US intelligence agencies should conduct surveillance while respecting the constitutional rights of US citizens; many of its recommendations have been adopted in laws, regulations, and policies. In the years since, civil liberties organizations and the government have continued to argue over the appropriate level of surveillance. But the 2016 attack in the US presidential campaign didn't come from US intelligence agencies; it came from the Russian government. What, if anything, can the US government do to prevent foreign agents from attacking its own citizens?

The Russians' strategic objective in disrupting democratic elections is not clear. But their actions exposed the soft underbelly of US civil society—and not just against the threat of attack by Russia. In the presence of such a ruthless enemy, anyone who participates in political activities and civil society needs access to the same sort of protections that journalists, human rights workers, and members of the national security establishment use to protect their communications and their data: end-to-end encrypted communications, secured phones, and two-factor authentication. In today's world, we need that security.

The encryption debate is not really about balancing public safety, national security, and privacy. It's about balancing law enforcement's easier access to evidence with society's need for strong online security. An NSA colleague once said that his agency has the right to break into certain systems, but no right that it be easy to do so. The criminal justice system would do well to keep that in mind.

It's time to take a step back and reflect on government's role in security. My state, Massachusetts, has the oldest surviving written constitution in the world. Ratified in 1780, this constitution predates the US Constitution by eight years. Article X of the Massachusetts document makes clear the state's responsibility for security:

> Each individual of the society has a right to be protected by it in the enjoyment of his life, liberty and property, according to standing laws.[33]

But Massachusetts, the site of many of the actions that led to the Revolutionary War, was a rebellious place, and its leaders were very concerned about protecting the individual against the state. Thus the state constitution also contains Article XIV:

> Every subject has a right to be secure from all unreasonable searches, and seizures, of his person, his houses, his papers, and all his possessions. All warrants, therefore, are contrary to this right, if the cause or foundation of them be not previously supported by oath or affirmation; and if the order in the warrant to a civil officer, to make search in suspected places, or to arrest one or more suspected persons, or to seize their property, be not accompanied with a special designation of the persons or objects of search, arrest, or seizure: and no warrant ought to be issued but in cases, and with the formalities prescribed by the laws.

If that article looks at all familiar, it should; it served as the basis for the Fourth Amendment in the US Bill of Rights. In that version, the restriction is simplified:

> The right of the people to be secure in their persons, houses, papers, and effects, against unreasonable searches and seizures, shall not be violated, and no Warrants shall issue, but upon probable cause, supported by Oath or affirmation, and particularly describing the place to be searched, and the persons or things to be seized.[34]

The tension between these two competing state needs—to protect the individual to enable her to enjoy her life, liberty, and property, but also to secure her against unreasonable searches and seizures—is still in play today. Balanced properly, this dynamic protects individuals and society, and enable both to thrive.

The Digital Revolution upended what needs securing and how to secure it. No one would deny that governments have a role in cybersecurity. The US-China agreement is an example of a positive step in cybersecurity that only governments can make happen. But bits play intimate roles in people's political, personal, and business lives. Unless the government intends to intervene in the minutiae of people's daily lives—which is so far not the case in the United States (or in any nation that has strong laws protecting the privacy and security of its citizens)—the government cannot be ultimately responsible for securing the bits. That's simply too invasive a role. Individuals and the private sector must be. And they must have the tools to do so.

Smartphones and other forms of electronic communication are now necessary for daily life, but they are not—as yet—secure. No device so essential to daily life, to financial transactions, to national security should be able to be turned into an eavesdropping system with ease. And the only way to prevent this is to make both the mode of communication and the devices themselves secure. The more secure communications and smartphones are, the more secure and private all of us are.

And that, in a nutshell, is it. The government's role is to provide security—national security and law enforcement—and not to prevent individuals from maintaining their own security. In a world surrounded by networked smart devices and increasingly capable adversaries, the government's responsibility is to protect us—and to enable us to secure ourselves.[35]

Notes

Preface

1. "The Encryption Tightrope: Balancing Americans' Security and Privacy," Hearing before the House Committee on the Judiciary, 114th Congress (2016; statement of Susan Landau, professor, Worcester Polytechnic Institute), 104–30.

2. "Surely the FBI": Steven M. Bellovin et al., "Lawful Hacking: Using Existing Vulnerabilities for Wiretapping on the Internet," *Northwestern Journal of Technology and Intellectual Property*, Vol. 12, Issue 1 (2014).

3. Eric Lipton, David Sanger, and Scott Shane, "The Perfect Weapon: How Russian Cyberpower Invaded the US," *New York Times*, December 13, 2016.

4. Evan Osnos, David Remnick, and Joshua Yaffa, "Trump, Putin, and the New Cold War," *New Yorker*, March 6, 2017.

5. "Now it was": Steven Adair, "PowerDuke: Widespread Post-Election Spear Phishing Campaigns Targeting Think Tanks and NGOs," Volexity, accessed March 3, 2017, https://www.volexity.com/blog/2016/11/09/powerduke -post-election-spear-phishing-campaigns-targeting-think-tanks-and-ngos/, November 9, 2016.

1
Racing into the Digital Revolution

1. "and 3D printers": Edward Tayler and Andreas Cremer, "Daimler Trucks to Use 3D Printing in Spare Parts Reduction," Reuters, July 13, 2016, accessed September 10, 2016, http://www.reuters.com/article/us-daimler -3dprinting-idUSKCN0ZT20.

2. The anti-aircraft targeting computers were analog machines. For information on Colossus, see Stephen Budiansky, *Battle of Wits: The Complete Story of Codebreaking in World War II* (New York: Simon and Schuster, 2000), 315.

3. "in the 1980s": Lotus 123, a spreadsheet program, was the "killer app" for the IBM PC.

4. "The populations of": Jacob Poushter, Pew Research Center, "Smartphone Ownership and Internet Usage Continue to Climb in Emerging Economies," February 22, 2016, accessed September 14, 2016, http://www.pewglobal.org/2016/02/22/smartphone-ownership-and-internet-usage-continue-to-climb-in-emerging-economies/.

5. For information on automation, see Mark Muro and Siddharth Kulkarni, "Voter Anger Explained—in One Chart," *The Avenue*, Brookings Institution, March 15, 2016, accessed February 28, 2017, https://www.brookings.edu/blog/the-avenue/2016/03/15/voter-anger-explained-in-one-chart/; Mark Muro, "It Won't Be Easy to Bring Back Millions of Manufacturing Jobs," *The Avenue*, Brookings Institution, November 18, 2016, accessed February 28, 2017, https://www.brookings.edu/blog/the-avenue/2016/11/18/it-wont-be-easy-to-bring-back-millions-of-manufacturing-jobs/.

6. "Encryption on its": Like any complex security threat, the cybersecurity problem can't be "solved," it can be only be managed. "Indeed, a leaked": James Ball, "Secret US Cybersecurity Report: Encryption Vital to Protect Data," *Guardian*, January 15, 2015. "The report concluded": Ball, "Secret US Cybersecurity Report."

7. "Members of the": Charles Arthur, "Which Phones Do World Leaders Use?" *Guardian*, March 28, 2014. "And in 2009": Jeff Zeleny, "For a High-Tech President, a Hard Fought E-Victory," *New York Times*, January 22, 2009. In 2016 the president's BlackBerry was replaced by a phone of limited value, one that "doesn't take pictures, . . . can't text, the phone doesn't work, . . . can't play . . . music," Trevor Mogg, "Obama Has Finally Ditched His BlackBerry, but Its Replacement Will Surprise You," *Yahoo! Tech*, June 12, 2016. "But from its": Statista.com, "Global Market Share Held by RIM Smartphones," accessed September 15, 2016, http://www.statista.com/statistics/263439/global-market-share-held-by-rim-smartphones/.

8. For readers of a certain age, the "eighteen-minute gap" is reminiscent of a different case during the Nixon administration; that gap, however, was eighteen and a half minutes long. David Kopel, "The Missing 18 1/2 Minutes: Presidential Destruction of Incriminating Evidence," *Washington Post*, June 16, 2014.

9. Apple Inc., *iOS Security: iOS 9.0 or Later*, September 2015, 4, accessed

March 22, 2017, https://ssl.apple.com/euro/privacy/d/generic/docs/iOS_Se
curity_Guide.pdf.

10. Apple's view is stated in Theodore J. Boutrous, Jr., Nicola T.
Hanna, Eric Vandevelde, Gibson, Dunn and Crutcher, Theodore Olson, Gibson,
Dunn and Crutcher, Marc Zwillinger, Jeffrey Landis, and Zwillgen PLLC,
Attorneys for Apple, *In the Matter of the Search of an Apple iPhone Seized
During an Execution of a Search Warrant on a Black Lexus IS300, California
License Plate 35KGD203*, US District Court, Central District of California,
Eastern Division (2016). Public opinion is discussed in Michael Shear,
David Sanger, and Katie Benner, "In the Apple Case, a Debate over Data
Hits Home," *New York Times*, March 13, 2016; and Pew Research Center,
"More Support for Justice Department than for Apple in Dispute over Un-
locking iPhone," February 22, 2016, accessed September 19, 2016, http://
www.people-press.org/2016/02/22/more-support-for-justice-department
-than-for-apple-in-dispute-over-unlocking-iphone/.

11. "In the mid-2000s": Richard George (former technical director for
information assurance, National Security Agency), in discussion with the
author, December 1, 2011.

12. In 2006, the FBI prevailed in making "facilities-based broadband
providers" subject to CALEA. Such providers may use Internet communications to transmit communications within their own facilities, but use old-
fashioned telephone service for connections to the user.

13. "Many nations with": John C. Coffee, Jr., "Law and the Market: The
Impact of Enforcement," *University of Pennsylvania Law Review*, Vol. 156
(2007), 229–311.

14. "The instant messages": CBS Television, *60 Minutes*, "A Rare Look at
How Insider Trading Works," May 22, 2016. "'She worked at Galleon'":
George Packer, "A Dirty Business: New York City's Top Prosecutor Takes On
Wall Street Crime," *New Yorker*, June 27, 2011.

15. "The evidence worked": Packer, "A Dirty Business." "In large part":
"Preet Bharara's Key Insider Trading Cases," *New York Times*, October 6,
2015; New York Field Office, FBI, "Hedge Fund Billionaire Raj Rajaratnam
Found Guilty in Manhattan Federal Court of Insider Trading Charges," May
11, 2011, and related court filings.

16. "But the closed-circuit": "Police Issue CCTV Images of London
Bombers," October 20, 2016, http://www.gettyimages.com/event/police
-issue-cctv-images-of-london-bombers-53265288#in-this-composite-of
-handout-images-released-friday-july-22-2005-by-picture-id53270554/.

17. "But Omar didn't": Sandra Laville, "Caught on Camera: Bomb Plot
Suspect Disguised Day after July 21," *Guardian*, February 20, 2007; and Jason

Burke, Anushka Asthana, Mark Townsend, Martin Bright, Tony Thompson, Tariq Bibi, and Barbara McMahon, "Run to Ground," *Guardian*, July 30, 2005. "Authorities caught up": Burke et al., "Run to Ground."

18. "After his bomb": Duncan Gardham, "Wife of July 21 Bomber Hussain Oman Guilty of Helping Him Escape," *Telegraph*, June 11, 2008. "At some point": Gardham, "Wife of July 21 Bomber."

19. "But he used": Karen McVeigh, "How CCTV Helped Snare Failed Terrorists," *Guardian*, July 10, 2007. "Law enforcement never": Kevin Sullivan, "From Refugee to Thug to Suspect in London Plot," *Washington Post*, August 4, 2005; and Ian Fisher and Alan Cowell, "Bombings in London: The Investigation: Suspect Held in Italy Said to Admit Carrying Bomb in Train," *New York Times*, July 31, 2005.

20. "On November 24": Mark Seal, "An Exclusive Look at Sony's Hacking Saga," *Vanity Fair*, February 24, 2015. "At the same": Seal, "An Exclusive Look at Sony's Hacking Saga"; and Kim Zetter, "Sony Got Hacked Hard: What We Know and Don't Know So Far," *WIRED*, December 3, 2014.

21. "In short, they": Seal, "An Exclusive Look at Sony's Hacking Saga"; and Steve Ragan, "Sony's IT Blueprints Leaked by Hackers," December 4, 2014, CSO, accessed October 8, 2015, http://www.csoonline.com/article/2855005/business-continuity/sonys-it-blueprints-leaked-by-hackers.html.

22. "The attackers": *BBC News*, "The Interview: A Guide to the Cyber Attack on Hollywood," December 29, 2014. "Sony's IT department": Kevin Mandia, chief operating officer, FireEye, on CBS Television, *60 Minutes*, "The Attack on Sony," April 12, 2015; and Peter Elind, "Inside the Hack: Part 1," *Forbes*, June 25, 2015.

23. "Employees set up": Michael Cieply and Brooks Barnes, "Sony Cyberattack, First a Nuisance, Grows into a Firestorm," *New York Times*, December 30, 2014.

24. "But as theaters": Cieply and Barnes, "Sony Cyberattack, First a Nuisance, Grows into a Firestorm." "President Obama stepped" and "Confirming that North": press conference, December 19, 2014.

25. "At first, some": NSA, "Is There 'Fifth Party' Collection?" accessed October 9, 2016, http://goodtimesweb.org/covert-operations/2015/media-35679.pdf/.

26. "Iran apparently responded": Nicole Perlroth, "In Cyberattack on Saudi Firm, U.S. Sees Iran Firing Back," *New York Times*, October 23, 2012. "Instead, Sony relied": Peter Elind, "Inside the Hack: Part 2," *Forbes*, June 26, 2015.

27. "Instead of storing": Peter Elind, "Inside the Hack: Part 3," *Forbes*, June 27, 2015.

28. "Late on the": Industrial Control Systems Cyber Emergency Response Team, "Alert (IR-ALERT-H-16-056-01)," February 25, 2016, accessed October 10, 2016. "Hackers disconnected at": SANS Industrial Control Systems and Electricity Information Sharing and Analysis Center, "Analysis of the Cyber Attack on the Ukrainian Power Grid: Defense Use Case," March 18, 2016, 11, http://www.nerc.com/pa/CI/ESISAC/Documents/E-ISAC_SANS_Ukraine_DUC_18Mar2016.pdf; and Kim Zetter, "Inside the Cunning, Unprecedented Hack of Ukraine's Power Grid," WIRED, March 3, 2016. "The attackers took": Electricity Information Sharing and Analysis Center, "Analysis of the Cyber Attack," 12–13.

29. "Someone sent company": SANS Industrial Control Systems and Electricity Information Sharing and Analysis Center, "Analysis of the Cyber Attack," 11.

30. "They did so": SANS Industrial Control Systems and Electricity Information Sharing and Analysis Center, "Analysis of the Cyber Attack," 7.

31. "But the thousands": Kim Zetter, "Inside the Cunning, Unprecedented Hack of Ukraine's Power Grid."

32. "The Ukrainian power": SANS Industrial Control Systems and Electricity Information Sharing and Analysis Center, "Analysis of the Cyber Attack," 3.

33. "Instead, employees of": SANS Industrial Control Systems and Electricity Information Sharing and Analysis Center, "Analysis of the Cyber Attack," 3.

2

We're All Connected Now

1. "Large organizations, including": Vivek Kundra, "Federal Cloud Computing Strategy," February 8, 2011, accessed May 14, 2017, https://www.dhs.gov/sites/default/files/publications/digital-strategy/federal-cloud-computing-strategy.pdf; and Barb Darrow, "Why the US Government Finally Loves Cloud Computing," Forbes, September 2, 2016.

2. "In November 2016": Detailed stats, Rosetta@home, accessed November 1, 2016, http://boincstats.com/en/stats/14/project/detail.

3. "Between 2011 and": Telegeography, Global Bandwidth Research Service, accessed October 19, 2016, https://www.telegeography.com/research-services/global-bandwidth-research-service/. "As I write": Internet World Stats, accessed November 1, 2016, http://www.internetworldstats.com/emarketing.htm.

4. "But in 1972": Laura Rocchio, National Aeronautics and Space Administration, "Landsat: Protecting the Price of Bread," April 2, 2007, accessed March 14, 2017, https://landsat.gsfc.nasa.gov/landsat-protecting-the-price -of-bread/.

5. "Machines that make": NASA, "Machine Shop," April 22, 2014, accessed October 20, 2016, https://www.nasa.gov/centers/armstrong/capabili ties/CodeZ/facilities/machine_shop.html.

6. "But automatic reporting": Dave Edstrom, "With Machine Monitoring, Instant ROI Is Possible," August 18, 2016, accessed October 26, 2016, http:// advancedmanufacturing.org/machine-monitoring-instant-roi-possible/. "Networking the full": Dave Edstrom, *MTConnect: To Measure Is to Know* (Ashburn, VA: Virtual PhotonsElectrons, 2013), 114–15. "Such simple changes": Marc Lobit, "Entering a New Information Age for Machine Utilization," *Canadian Industrial Machinery Magazine*, July 7, 2015.

7. "When a sensor": Cisco, "Discover FANUC ZDT: Zero Downtime," accessed December 17, 2016, http://motioncontrolsrobotics.com/discover -fanuc-zdt-zero-downtime. "Service centers at": Frank Tobe, "Big Data, the Cloud . . . and FANUC and Kuka?" *Robot Report*, June 7, 2016, accessed October 20, 2016, https://www.therobotreport.com/news/big-data-the-cloud -and-fanuc-and-kuka.

8. " 'Rick Schneider, CEO' " and "Within six months": Rick Schneider, "FANUC Embraces IoT through Cisco Intercloud," accessed October 21, 2016, http://video.cisco.com/detail/videos/featured-videos/video/428932089 6001/fanuc-embraces-iot-through-cisco-intercloud.

9. "So the company": Jon Gertner, "Behind GE's Vision for the Industrial Internet of Things," *Fast Company*, June 18, 2014, accessed November 17, 2016, https://www.fastcompany.com/3031272/can-jeff-immelt-really-make -the-world-1-better; and GE, "The Case for an Industrial Big Data Platform: Laying the Groundwork for a New Industrial Age," 2013, accessed January 23, 2016, http://www.ge.com/digital/sites/default/files/Industrial_Big_Data _Platform.pdf.

10. "Each day, each": Gertner, "Behind GE's Vision for the Industrial Internet of Things. "Now those engines": Laura Winig, "GE's Big Bet on Data and Analytics," *MIT Sloan Management Review*, Vol. 17, Issue 3 (February 18, 2016).

11. "ready for breeding": Brian Barth, "Luddites Beware: These 5 Livestock Wearables Are the Future," *Modern Farmer*, January 28, 2016. "coming down with mastitis": M. L. Stangaferro et al., "Use of Rumination and Activity Monitoring for the Identification of Dairy Cows with Health Disorders.

Part II: Mastitis," *Journal of Dairy Science*, Vol. 99 (2016), 2,843–49, doi: http://dx.org/10.3168/jds2016-10907.

12. "Similar tools can": Juliana Lockman, Robert Fisher, and Donald Olson, "Detection of Seizure-like Movements Using a Wrist Accelerometer," *Epilepsy and Behavior*, Vol. 20, Issue 4 (April 2011), 638–41, doi: 10.1016/j .yebeh.2011.01.019.

13. "The community now": Marilyn Rantz et al., "Automated Technology to Speed Recognition of Signs of Illness in Older Adults," *Journal of Gerontological Nursing*, Vol. 38, No. 4 (April 2014), 18–23, doi: 10.3928 /00989134-20120307-01.

14. "Apple's ResearchKit turns": Apple, accessed March 18, 2017, https:// www.apple.com/researchkit/. "Over 9,000": Brian Bot et al., "The mPower Study, Parkinson Disease Mobile Data Collected Using ResearchKit," *Scientific Data*, Vol. 3 (2016), doi:10.1038/sdata.2016.11.

15. Originally, however, different railways did not connect in major cities. This explains the phenomenon of London's Waterloo, Victoria, Euston, Paddington, King's Cross, and St. Pancras railway stations, and Paris's Gare du Nord, Gare Montparnasse, Gare d'Austerlitz, Gare St. Lazare, and Gare de Lyon.

16. The first power plants used direct current (DC), which is problematic. That's because high-voltage lines are more efficient at power transmission, but DC cannot easily be increased in voltage. There's also less power loss when transmitting power over long distances if alternating current (AC) is used. But for various reasons, including an installed base that used DC, the transition to AC took decades.

17. "Each system consists": Committee on Enhancing the Robustness and Resilience of Future Electrical Transmission and Distribution in the United States to Terrorist Attack, National Research Council, *Terrorism and the Electric Power Supply* (Washington: National Academies Press, 2012), 21–22.

18. "The lesson was": U.S.-Canada Power System Outage Task Force, *Final Report on the August 14, 2003 Blackout in the United States and Canada: Causes and Recommendations* (April 2004), 45.

19. "Indeed, the US": Peter Daly, "Banking and Finance," accessed October 9, 2016, http://www.iwar.org.uk/cip/resources/pccip/acpdf/ac_bank.pdf.

20. Contactless cards have a chip and a small antenna. They communicate with a terminal via radio waves. "Increasingly, certain types": Megan Woolhouse, "No Cash Allowed: Stores Refusing to Accept Money," *Boston Globe*, August 4, 2016.

21. "Electronic money is": Geeta Anand and Hari Kumar, "India Hobbles through a Cash Crisis, and Electronic Payments Boom," *New York Times,* December 13, 2016.

22. "In Sweden, less": Jon Henley, "Sweden Leads the Race to Become a Cashless Society," *Guardian,* June 4, 2016. "Beggars in Stockholm": Gaby Hinsliff, "Are We Heading Towards a Cashless Future?" *Guardian Weekly,* October 28–November 3, 2016. "Denmark, Norway, and": Nathan Heller, "Letter from Stockholm: Imagining a Cashless World," *New Yorker,* October 10, 2016. "And the same": Anand and Kumar, "India Hobbles through a Cash Crisis."

23. "Unless the Google": smartray05, "Location History Sampling Info," December 11, 2012, accessed October 31, 2016, https://productforums.goo gle.com/forum/#!msg/maps/ldKaXij4c_0/qsnMfunamM4J.

24. "Through testing, the": M. J. Rantz et al., "A New Paradigm of Tech-nology-Enabled 'Vital Signs' for Early Detection of Health Change for Older Adults," *Gerontology,* Vol. 61, No. 3 (2015), doi: 10.1159/000366518.

25. "The company has": StatisticBrain, "FedEx Company Statistics," ac-cessed October 31, 2016, http://www.statisticbrain.com/fedex-company -statistics/.

26. "In the United": Federal Railroad Administration, US Department of Transportation, "Freight Rail Today," accessed October 31, 2016, https:// www.fra.dot.gov/Page/P0362. "Broken rails or": X. Liu, M. R. Saat, and C. P. L. Barkan, "Analysis of Causes of Major Train Derailments and Their Ef-fect on Accident Rates," *Transportation Research Record* 2289 (2012), 154–63.

27. "The result is": Gertner, "Behind GE's Vision for the Industrial Inter-net of Things," and GE, "The Case for an Industrial Big Data Platform."

28. I am indebted to Hal Stern for the heavy metal example.

3

Dangers Lurking Within

1. "The first night": US Department of Defense, *Annual Report on the Military Power of the People's Republic of China,* FY04 Report to Congress on PRC Military Power, Pursuant to the FY2000 National Defense Authoriza-tion Act, 19, accessed November 10, 2016, http://archive.defense.gov/pubs /d20040528PRC.pdf.

2. "Instead, defense experts": US Department of Defense, *Annual Report on the Military Power of the People's Republic of China,* 24.

3. " 'They never hit' ": Nathan Thornburgh, "Inside the Chinese Hack At-

tack: How a Ring of Hackers, Codenamed Titan Rain by Investigators, Probed U.S. Government Computers," *Time,* August 25, 2005. "The attackers got": Thornburgh, "Inside the Chinese Hack Attack"; and Nathan Thornburgh, "The Invasion of the Chinese Cyberspies (and the Man Who Tried to Stop Them)," *Time,* September 25, 2005. "The bits disappeared": Thornburgh, "Inside the Chinese Hack Attack."

4. "The hackers successfully": John Markoff, "Cyberattack on Google Said to Hit Password System," *New York Times,* April 20, 2014; David Drummond, "A New Approach to China," Google Official Blog, January 12, 2010, accessed November 12, 2016, https://googleblog.blogspot.com/2010/01/new-approach-to-china.html; Ellen Nakashima, "Chinese Hackers Who Breached Google Gained Access to Sensitive Data, US Officials Say," *Washington Post,* May 20, 2013. "They had also breached Gmail": Drummond, "A New Approach to China."

5. "Hacker targets included": Drummond, "A New Approach to China"; Kim Zetter, "Google Hackers Targeted Source Code of More Than 30 Companies," *WIRED,* January 13, 2010; Arian Eunjung Cja and Ellen Nakishima, "Google China Cyberattack Part of Vast Espionage Campaign, Experts Say," *Washington Post,* January 14, 2010; Fahmida Rashid, "HBGary E-mail says DuPont Hit by Operation Aurora's Email Attack," EWEEK.COM (March 3, 2011), http://www.eweek.com/c/a/Security/HBGary-Emails-Say-DuPont-Hit-by-Chinas-Operation-Aurora-Attack-306724/.

6. "The Department of": Reuters, "Theft of F-35 Design Data Is Helping Adversaries—Pentagon," June 19, 2013, accessed November 14, 2016, http://www.reuters.com/article/usa-fighter-hacking-idUSL2N0EV0T320130619. "Later, the Snowden": Sasha Goldstein, "Chinese Hackers Stole F-35 Fighter Jet Blueprints in Pentagon Hack, Edward Snowden Documents Claim," *New York Daily News,* January 20, 2015; and NSA, "Chinese Exfiltrate Sensitive Military Technology," *Spiegel,* accessed November 14, 2016, http://www.spiegel.de/media/media-35687.pdf. "Years later, when": Marcus Weisgerber, "China's Copycat Jet Raises Questions about F-35," *DefenseOne,* September 23, 2015, accessed November 14, 2016, http://www.defenseone.com/threats/2015/09/more-questions-f-35-after-new-specs-chinas-copycat/121859/.

7. "Seventy percent of" and "Chinese hackers sought": "Digital Spying Burdens German-Chinese Relations," *Spiegel Online,* February 25, 2013, accessed November 14, 2016, http://www.spiegel.de/international/world/digital-spying-burdens-german-relations-with-beijing-a-885444.html.

8. "Between 2006 and" and "The types of data": Dmitri Alperovitch, "Revealed: Operation Shady Rat," 2011, 7–9, http://www.mcafee.com/us

/resources/white-papers/wp-operation-shady-rat.pdf. "An NSA briefing":
NBC Nightly News with Lester Holt, "Stunning Map Shows Chinese Cyber
Spies Target US Hundreds of Times," July 30, 2015. "more romantically if":
Brian McKenna, "What Does a Petabyte Look Like?" ComputerWeekly.com,
March 2013, accessed April 4, 2017, http://www.computerweekly.com/fea
ture/What-does-a-petabyte-look-like.

9. "Apparently, so were": Defense Security Service, US Department of
Defense, "Targeting US Technologies: A Trend Analysis of Cleared Industry
Reporting," 2014.

10. "Or, as in": Kim Zetter, "Inside the Cunning, Unprecedented Hack of
Ukraine's Power Grid," *WIRED,* March 3, 2016.

11. Dennis Blair, "Annual Threat Assessment for the Intelligence Community for the Senate Select Committee on Intelligence," February 12, 2009,
accessed March 22, 2017, http://www.circleofblue.org/wp-content/uploads
/2012/03/DNI_threat-assessment-2009.pdf, 28; Dennis Blair, "Annual Threat
Assessment for the Intelligence Community for the Senate Select Committee on Intelligence," February 2, 2010, accessed March 22, 2017, www
.dtic.mil/cgi-bin/GetTRDoc?AD=ADA514221; James Clapper, "Unclassified
Statement for the Record on the Worldwide Threat Assessment of the US
Intelligence Community for the House Permanent Select Committee on Intelligence," February 10, 2011, accessed March 22, 2017, http://www.au.af
.mil/au/awc/awcgate/dni/threat_assessment_10feb11.pdf, 26; James Clapper,
"Unclassified Statement for the Record on the Worldwide Threat Assessment of the US Intelligence Community for the Senate Select Committee on
Intelligence," January 31, 2012, accessed March 22, 2017, https://www.dni
.gov/files/documents/Newsroom/Testimonies/20120131_testimony_ata
.pdf; James Clapper, "Statement for the Record: Worldwide Threat Assessment of the US Intelligence Community for the Senate Select Committee on
Intelligence," March 12, 2013, accessed March 22, 2017, https://www.dni
.gov/files/documents/Intelligence%20Reports/2013%20ATA%20SFR%20
for%20SSCI%2012%20Mar%202013.pdf; James Clapper, "Statement for the
Record: Worldwide Threat Assessment of the US Intelligence Community,
Senate Select Committee on Intelligence," January 29, 2014, accessed March
22, 2017, https://www.dni.gov/files/documents/Intelligence%20Reports/2014
%20WWTA%20%20SFR_SSCI_29_Jan.pdf; James Clapper, "Statement for
the Record: Worldwide Threat Assessment of the US Intelligence Community," February 26, 2015, accessed March 22, 2017, https://www.dni.gov
/index.php/newsroom/congressional-testimonies/congressional-testimonies
-2015/item/1174-statement-for-the-record-worldwide-threat-assessment
-of-the-u-s-ic-before-the-senate-armed-services-committee; James Clapper,

"Statement for the Record: Worldwide Threat Assessment of the US Intelligence Community, Senate Armed Services Committee" February 9, 2016, accessed March 22, 2017, https://www.armed-services.senate.gov/imo/media/doc/Clapper_02-09-16.pdf.

12. "Stoll began to": Cliff Stoll, *Cuckoo's Egg: Stalking the Wily Hacker* (New York: Doubleday, 1989), 23–25. "Stoll watched him": Stoll, *Cuckoo's Egg*, 40.

13. "The Bureau scoffed": Stoll, *Cuckoo's Egg*, 35.

14. "But Morris had": Donn Seely, "A Tour of the Worm," University of Utah Computer Science Department Technical Report, November 1988. "Systems were dropping": John Markoff, "'Virus' in Computer Network Disrupts Systems Nationwide," *New York Times*, November 4, 1988.

15. "DARPA, the US": US Government Accountability Office, *Virus Highlights Need for Improved Internet Management*, IMTEC-89-57, June 12, 1989.

16. "If Stoll's intruder": Stoll, *Cuckoo's Egg*, 96–97.

17. These hashes were computed using SHA256.

18. "The sites that": F. T. Grampp and R. H. Morris, "UNIX Operating System Security," *AT&T Bell Laboratories Technical Journal*, Vol. 63, No. 8 (October 1984), 1,653–54.

19. "As a US": US Government Accountability Office, *Virus Highlights Need for Improved Internet Management*, 19–20.

20. "As of this": Internet World Stats, "History and Growth of the Internet from 1995 til Today," accessed November 28, 2016, http://www.internetworldstats.com/emarketing.htm.

21. "A few companies": In part, this was the result of a conscious decision by Amazon's CEO to grow the company slowly.

22. "Hackers' forays into": James Adams, "Virtual Defense," *Foreign Affairs*, May–June 2001; "Cyberwar! The Warnings?" PBS *Frontline*, April 24, 2003, accessed November 29, 2016, http://www.pbs.org/wgbh/pages/frontline/shows/cyberwar/warnings/.

23. The viruses did further damage as well. Melissa infected Word documents on the computer's hard drive and mailed those out, while ILOVEYOU sent users and passwords on the infected machine back to the virus's author, as well as overwriting MP3 and jpg files.

24. One reason for the severity of the IIS problem is that many laptop and desktop machines were, unknown to the owner, running IIS. This was because some applications wanted a webserver—so they turned it on. "Then the worm": David Moore, Colleen Shannon, and k. claffy, "Code-red: A Case Study on the Spread and Victims of an Internet Worm," *IMW'02 Proceedings of the Second SIGCOMM Workshop on Internet Measurement*, November 6–8, 2002, 273–84.

25. "What Can Be Done to Reduce the Threats Posed by Computer Viruses and Worms to the Workings of the Government?" Hearing before the House Subcommittee on Government Efficiency, Financial Management, and Government Relations of the Committee on Government Reform, 107th Congress (2001; statement by Keith Rhodes, chief technologist, General Accounting Office).

26. "By the time": Steve Lipner (retired; formerly partner director of Software Security, Trustworthy Computing, Microsoft), in discussion with the author, December 2, 2016. "Indeed, Microsoft's Security": Microsoft, "Security Development Lifecycle," accessed November 30, 2016, https://www.microsoft.com/security/sdl/story/.

27. In discussing crimes that came about as a result of the Digital Revolution, I am omitting the fights between the music industry and users over the use of peer-to-peer file sharing systems such as Napster (there are two systems named Napster, the peer-to-peer file and a later instantiation of it as an online music store). This dispute has been largely resolved through the licensing model for music.

28. "Others placed packet": James Vereni, "The Great Cyberheist," *New York Times,* November 10, 2010; and Kim Zetter, "TJX Hacker Gets 20 Years in Prison," *WIRED,* March 25, 2010. "The thefts were": Zetter, "TJX Hacker Gets 20 Years in Prison." "The illegal tap": Jaiykumar Vijayan, "SQL Injection Attacks Led to Heartland, Hannaford Breaches," *Computerworld,* August 18, 2009.

29. "They withdrew money": US Department of Justice, Office of Public Affairs, "Alleged International Hacking Ring Caught in $9 Million Fraud," November 10, 2009; and US District Court, Northeastern District of Georgia, Atlanta Division, *United States v. Viktor Pleshchuk, Sergei Turikov, Hacker 3, Oleg Covelin, Igor Grudijev, Ronald Tsoi, Evelin Tsoi, and Mithail Jevgenov, Defendants, Criminal Indictment 1-09-CR-491* (November 10, 2009), 3–5.

30. "The US Department": US District Court, District of Massachusetts, *United States of America v. Albert Gonzalez, Defendant, Criminal No. 08-CR-10223-PBS, Criminal No. 09-CR-10262-PBS, Criminal No. 09-CR-10382-DPW* (redacted version), Government's Sentencing Memorandum, 5. "For example, the": Dinei Florencio and Cormac Herley, "Sex, Lies and Cyber Crime Surveys," *Workshop in Economics of Information Security and Privacy,* 2011, 50. "A more reliable": Richard Sullivan, "The Changing Nature of US Card Payment Fraud: Industry and Public Policy Options," *Economic Review,* Vol. 95, No. 2 (2010), 101–33.

31. "Russian websites urged": Kertu Ruus, "Cyber War I: Estonia Attacked from Russia," *European Affairs,* Vol. 9, Issue 1–2 (Winter/Spring 2008), http://

www.europeaninstitute.org/index.php/component/content/article?id=67
:cyber-war-i-estonia-attacked-from-russia.

32. "They launched at": Dan Holden, "Estonia, Six Years Later," Arbor Networks, May 16, 2013, accessed December 1, 2016, https://www.arbornet works.com/blog/asert/estonia-six-years-later/. "Soon the engineers": Joshua Davis, "Hackers Take Down the Most Wired Country in Europe," *WIRED*, August 21, 2007.

33. "NATO concluded": Eneken Tikk, Kadri Kaska, and Liss Vihul, *International Cyber Incidents: Legal Considerations* (Tallinn: Cooperative Cyber Defence Center of Excellence, 2010), 23–24.

34. "Within a day": Michael Schwirtz, Anne Barnard, and C. J. Chivers, "Russia and Georgia Clash over Separatist Region," *New York Times*, August 8, 2008.

35. "The combination meant": Ronald Diebert, Rafal Rohozinski, and Masahi Crete-Nishihata, "Cyclones in Cyberspace: Information-shaping and Denial in the Russia–Georgia War," *Security Dialogue*, Vol. 43, No. 1 (2012), 12.

36. "The attacks were": Diebert et al., "Cyclones in Cyberspace," 16–17. "The botnets were": Joel Hruska, "Russians May Not Be Responsible for Cyberattacks on Georgia," *arstechnica*, August 13, 2008.

37. "By 2006, Iran": "Iran-IAEA: Israeli Atomic Energy Commission Reviews Israel's Discussion with Russia," February 15, 2006, accessed December 2, 2016, https://wikileaks.org/plusd/cables/06TELAVIV688_a.html. "In 2009, odd": Kim Zetter, *Countdown to Zero Day: Stuxnet and the Launch of the World's First Digital Weapon* (New York: Crown, 2014), 1–2. "An uninterruptable power": Kim Zetter, *Countdown to Zero Day*, 200–201. "The centrifuges began": Zetter, *Countdown to Zero Day*, 3.

38. "The network running": Zetter, *Countdown to Zero Day*, 227, 302, and 233–39. "This was, in": Zetter, *Countdown to Zero Day*, 28–29.

39. "Two of the": Zetter, *Countdown to Zero Day*, 90 and 93. "The fifth also": Zetter, *Countdown to Zero Day*, 278. "Stuxnet used stolen": Zetter, *Countdown to Zero Day*, 11–12 and 16.

40. "Stuxnet's precise targeting": Zetter, *Countdown to Zero Day*, 173–79; and Frank Rieger, "Knowledge Brings Fear," September 22, 2010, accessed December 31, 2016, http://frank.geekheim.de/?p=1189. "Shortly thereafter, workers": Zetter, *Countdown to Zero Day*, 238.

41. "Over time the": David Sanger, "Obama Order Sped Up Wave of Cyberattacks Against Iran," *New York Times*, June 1, 2012. "In August 2012": Dan Goodin, "Mystery Malware Wreaks Havoc on Energy Sector Computers," *arstechnica*, August 16, 2012. "The virus did": Nicole Perlroth, "In Cy-

berattack on Saudi Firm, US Sees Iran Firing Back," *New York Times,* October 23, 2012.

42. "Sony and the": Benjamin Elgin and Michael Riley, "Nuke Remark Stirred Attack on Sands Casinos that Foreshadowed Sony," *Bloomberg Technology,* December 11, 2014, accessed December 3, 2016, https://www.bloom berg.com/news/articles/2014-12-11/nuke-remark-stirred-hack-on-sands -casinos-that-foreshadowed-sony; James Clapper, "Worldwide Threat Assessment of the US Intelligence Committee: Hearing before Senate Armed Forces Committee" (2015).

43. "In 2013 the": Mandiant, "APT1: Exposing One of China's Cyberespionage Units," 2013. "The US government": Office of Public Affairs, US Department of Justice, "US Charges Five Military Hackers for Cyber Espionage Against US Corporations and a Labor Organization for Commercial Advantage," May 19, 2014, accessed December 7, 2016, https://www.justice.gov /opa/pr/us-charges-five-chinese-military-hackers-cyber-espionage-against -us-corporations-and-labor.

44. "Merkel, normally a": Ian Traynor and Paul Lewis, "Merkel Compared NSA to Stasi in Heated Encounter with Obama," *Guardian,* December 17, 2013.

45. "In the summer": US District Court, Southern District of New York, Ahmad Fathi, Hamid Firoozi, Amin Shokohi, Sadegh Ahmadzadegan, a/k/a "Nitrojen26," Omid Ghaffarinia, a/k/a "PLuS," Sina Keissar, and Nader Saedi, a/k/a "Turk Server," Defendants, Sealed Indictment, 14–15, accessed December 4, 2016, https://www.justice.gov/opa/file/834996/download. "The dam controls" and "Or had the": Joseph Berger, "A Dam, Small and Unsung, Is Caught Up in an Iranian Hacking Case," *New York Times,* March 25, 2016.

46. "In 2014, Vietnam": Crowdstrike, "Global Threat Intel Report," 2014, 9, https://go.crowdstrike.com/rs/281-OBQ-266/images/ReportGlobalThreat Intelligence.pdf?aliId=3920558. "China appeared to": Crowdstrike, "Global Threat Intel Report," 42.

47. "The credential apparently" and "After that, the": Brendan Koerner, "Inside the Cyberattack that Shocked the US Government," *WIRED,* October 23, 2016.

48. "Point-of-sale": Auriemma Consulting Group, "Counterfeit Credit Card Fraud Reaches Lowest Level Since 2013; Other Fraud Types Increase, Says Auriemma Consulting Group," July 7, 2016, accessed December 6, 2016, http://www.acg.net/counterfeit-credit-card-fraud-reaches-lowest-level -since-2013-other-fraud-types-increase-says-auriemma-consulting-group/. "Both account takeover": Auriemma Consulting Group and ThreatMetrix, *Q3 2016: Cybercrime Report,* 18. "Or, as one": ThreatMetrix, *Q3 2016,* 7.

49. "Consider Russia's theft": David Sanger and Charlie Savage, "US Says Russia Directed Hacks to Influence Elections," *New York Times*, October 7, 2016; Eric Lipton and Scott Shane, "Democratic House Candidates Were Also Targets of Russian Hacking," *New York Times*, December 13, 2016. "As the director": "Joint Statement from the Department of Homeland Security and Office of the Director of National Intelligence, of the Director of National Intelligence on Election Security," October 7, 2016, accessed December 9, 2016, https://www.dhs.gov/news/2016/10/07/joint-statement-department -homeland-security-and-office-director-national.

50. "Russia is employing": "United States Cyber Command," Hearing before the Senate Committee on Armed Services, 115th Congress (2017), Michael Rogers (testimony). "The same Russian": Alex Hern, "Macron Hackers Linked to Russian-Affiliated Group behind US Attack," *Guardian*, May 8, 2017. "Russia is believed": Melissa Eddy, "After a Cyberattack, Germany Fears Election Disruption," *New York Times*, December 8, 2016. "There are hints": Andrew Higgins, "Fake News, Fake Ukrainians: How a Group of Russians Tilted a Dutch Vote," *New York Times*, February 16, 2017.

4
How Do We Protect Ourselves?

1. George Tenet, "Information Security Risks, Opportunities, and the Bottom Line," Sam Nunn Nations Bank Policy Forum, Georgia Institute of Technology, April 6, 1998.

2. Richard Danzig, "Surviving on a Diet of Poisoned Fruit: Reducing the National Security Risks of America's Cyber Dependencies," Center for a New American Security, 2014, 6.

3. "Pieces of the": Kevin Hartnett, "Computer Scientists Close in on Perfect, Hack-Proof Code," *WIRED*, September 23, 2016.

4. "Even with more": Hartnett, "Computer Scientists Close in on Perfect, Hack-Proof Code."

5. "In some cases": In discussion with the author, November 9, 2016.

6. "There's no authentication," "Shared passwords are," and "The average factory": In discussion with the author. "Their response is": Ralph Langner and Perry Pederson, *Bound to Fail: Why Cyber Security Risk Cannot Simply Be "Managed" Away*, Computer Security Series, Brookings Institution, February 2013, 5.

7. "The chief of": Rob Joyce, "USENIX ENIGMA," https://www.youtube .com/watch?v=bDJb8WOJYdA, January 28, 2016.

8. "When the fight": Public Cryptography Study Group, *Report of the*

Public Cryptography Study Group, American Council on Education, Washington, DC, 1981; reprinted in *Notices of the American Mathematical Society,* October 1981, 518–26. "Later, the NSA": Computer Security Law of 1987, P.L. No. 100–235.

9. "In the 1990s": There were various exceptions, including for systems using encryption for authentication and integrity checking. Whitfield Diffie and Susan Landau, "The Export of Cryptography in the 20th Century and the 21st," *The History of Information Security: A Comprehensive Handbook,* ed. Karl De Leeuw and Jan Bergstra (Amsterdam: Elsevier, 2007), 725–36.

10. "In the Caesar": David Kahn, *The Codebreakers: The Comprehensive History of Secret Communication from Ancient Times to the Internet,* rev. ed. (New York: Scribner, 1996), 84.

11. "That's because the": Expressing a number in binary is expressing in base 2, where the only digits are 0s and 1s. Thus 25 in base 10 becomes 11,001 in base 2; this signifies 1x24+1x23+0x22+0x21+1x20. "One of the": This is the Advanced Encryption Standard; see http://csrc.nist.gov/publica tions/fips/fips197/fips-197.pdf.

12. "The security of": This is Kerckhoffs's Principle, named after the Dutch cryptographer who proposed it. See Auguste Kerckhoffs, "La cryptographie militaire," *Journal des sciences militaires,* Vol. 9 (1883), 5–83 and 161–91.

13. "When cryptography was": During World War II, the Soviet Union used a system called "one-time pad" that, as long as keys are used only once, is unbreakable. But the Soviet Union reused some of the keys. This enabled the United States to decrypt some of the encrypted messages, exposing Klaus Fuchs, a Soviet spy at the Manhattan Project, and Donald Maclean, one of the "Cambridge Five," as spies. See https://www.nsa.gov/news-features /declassified-documents/venona/.

14. "Their solution(s) relied": Diffie and Hellman showed how two parties, communicating over an insecure communications channel like the Internet— or even a wiretapped phone line—can exchange messages, allowing them to create a secret encryption key that no one else can discover. Ralph Merkle, an undergraduate at UC-Berkeley, independently invented public-key cryptography, but his method for key distribution was impractical. Whitfield Diffie and Martin Hellman, "New Directions in Cryptography," *IEEE Transactions in Information Theory,* Vol. 22, Issue 6 (1976), 644–54. James Ellis, Clifford Cocks, and Malcolm Williamson of GCHQ, the British signals-intelligence agency, had also discovered these ideas, but their work was not made public until 1997. The import of the work was not understood at the time; no use was made of it. James Ellis, *The Possibility of Secure Non-Secret Encryption,* Research Report No. 3006 (Cheltenham, UK: GCHQ/CESG, December 16, 1969).

15. This approach is the RSA algorithm: Ronald Rivest, Adi Shamir, and Leonard Adleman, "A Method for Obtaining Digital Signatures and Public Key Crypto-systems," *Communications of the ACM,* Vol. 21, Issue 2 (1978), 120–126, doi: 10.1145/359340.359342. "It would take": Digicert, "Check Our Numbers: The Math behind Estimations to Break a 2048-bit Certificate," accessed January 14, 2017, https://www.digicert.com/TimeTravel/math .htm. The US government allows systems with 128-bit keys for protecting secret documents, but public-key systems use much longer keys to achieve the same level of security as systems in which the sender and recipient share the same key. See Arjen Lenstra and Eric Verheul, "Selecting Cryptographic Key Sizes," *Journal of Cryptology,* Vol. 14, No. 4 (2001), 255–93, doi:10.1007 /s00145-001-0009-4.

16. The public key also includes an integer e that is easily calculated by the key's owner; the private key has a corresponding integer d also easily calculated by the public key's owner.

17. That would give": Brent Scowcroft, "Memorandum for the Honorable Dick Cheney, the Honorable William P. Barr, the Honorable Robert M. Gates," January 17, 1991, in Bruce Schneier and David Banisar, eds., *The Electronic Privacy Papers: Documents on the Battle for Privacy in the Age of Surveillance* (New York: John Wiley and Sons, 1997), 160.

18. "Around this time": "Encryption, Key Recovery, and Privacy Protection in the Information Age," Hearing before the Senate Judiciary Committee, 105th Congress (1997; statement of Louis Freeh, director of the FBI).

19. "Other nations balked": Whitfield Diffie and Susan Landau, *Privacy on the Line: The Politics of Wiretapping and Encryption,* rev. ed. (Cambridge, MA: MIT Press, 2007), 238–39.

20. "Instead of easing": Diffie and Landau, *Privacy on the Line,* 236–41.

21. "Throughout the following": Matt Apuzzo, "FBI Used Hacking Software Decade before iPhone Fight," *New York Times,* April 13, 2016.

22. "In the words": "The Encryption Tightrope: Balancing Americans' Security and Privacy," Hearing before the House Committee on the Judiciary, 114th Congress (2016; statement of James Comey, director of the FBI), 7. "My colleague Matt": Matt Blaze on *Last Week Tonight with John Oliver,* March 13, 2016, accessed January 16, 2017, https://www.youtube .com/watch?v=zsjZ2r9Ygzw, 12:15.

23. "Months before the": Mike McConnell, Michael Chertoff, and William Lynn III, "Why the Fear over Ubiquitous Data Encryption Is Overblown," *Washington Post,* July 28, 2015. "Another former NSA": Marc Thiessen and Michael Hayden, "General Michael Hayden on Apple, the FBI, and Data Encryption," American Enterprise Institute, March 23, 2016, accessed

January 7, 2017, https://www.aei.org/publication/gen-michael-hayden-on
-apple-the-fbi-and-data-encryption/.

24. "While the intelligence": Hearing on Foreign Cyber Threats to the
United States before the Senate Committee on Armed Services, 115th Con-
gress (2017; statement of James Clapper, director of national intelligence).
"The exceptional access": The discussion on security problems of excep-
tional access is based on Harold Abelson et al., "Keys under Doormats:
Mandating Insecurity by Requiring Government Access to All Data and
Communications," *Journal of Cybersecurity*, Vol. 1, No. 1 (2015), doi: https://
doi.org/10.1093/cybsec/tyv009.

25. "Even decades-old": NSA, Venona, May 3, 2016, accessed January 13,
2017, https://www.nsa.gov/news-features/declassified-documents/venona/.

26. "A concept known": Whitfield Diffie, Paul von Oorschot, and Michael
Wiener, "Authentication and Authenticated Key Exchanges," *Designs, Codes,
and Cryptography*, Vol. 2, No. 2 (1992), 107–25, doi: 10.1007/BF00124891.
"It's the technology": Electronic Frontier Foundation, "Secure Messaging
Scorecard," accessed January 12, 2017, https://www.eff.org/node/82654; and
Christina Garman et al., "Dancing on the Lip of a Volcano: Chosen Cipher-
text Attacks on Apple's iMessage," 25th USENIX Security Symposium, 2016.
"As of January": Trustworthy Internet, "Building Together a Trustworthy
Internet: One Project at a Time," accessed January 12, 2017, https://www
.trustworthyinternet.org/ssl-pulse/.

27. "The researchers found": This is known as the FREAK—Factoring
RSA_Export Keys—Attack. See Benjamin Beurdouche et al., "A Messy State
of the Union: Taming the Composite State Machines of TLS," 2015 Symposium on IEEE Security and Privacy, doi: 10.1109/SP.2015.39

28. "During the First": Diffie and Landau, *Privacy on the Line*, 238–39.

29. "In 1996, a": Kenneth Dam and Herbert Lin, *Cryptography's Role in
Securing the Information Society* (Washington, DC: National Academies
Press, 1996), 11.

30. "The language has": "Ninishghal" means "I finished eating it." The
verb stem *ghal* denotes a circular action, such as moving the jaw while eating
meat. The prefix *sh-* means "I," while the prefix *ni* that comes right before
sh- means "finished." The first prefix *ni-* distinguishes this verb from others
involving circular actions, such as "hinishghal," which means "I arrived
wriggling." Margaret Speas (professor, Department of Linguistics, University of Massachusetts at Amherst), in discussion with the author, January 11,
2017. "The code replaced": Sarah Hoagland Hunter, *The Unbreakable Code*
(Flagstaff, AZ: Rising Moon Books, 1996).

31. "The difficulty of": Kahn, *The Codebreakers*, 550.

32. "Navajo code talkers": Roy Hawthorne in Nathan Aaseng, *Navajo Code Talkers: America's Secret Weapon in World War II* (New York: Walker, 1992), viii. "The shelling stopped": Aaseng, *Navajo Code Talkers*, 1–3.

33. "The bank eventually": Randal Gainer, "$90 Million Cyber Thefts from Banks Using SWIFT Network Raise Security Issues," *Data Privacy Monitor*, July 7, 2016; Sergei Shevchenko, "Two Bytes to $951 Million," BAE Systems Threat Research Blog, April 25, 2016, accessed March 19, 2017, https://baesystemsai.blogspot.de/2016/04/two-bytes-to-951m.html.

34. "SWIFT responded by": SWIFT, Customer Security Program, accessed January 9, 2017, https://www.swift.com/myswift/customer-security-programme-csp_/security-controls#topic-tabs-menu.

35. "In 2011, when": Less than 40 percent of the US population had smartphones in 2011 (and the numbers were lower almost everywhere else); Aaron Smith, "Overview of Smartphone Adoption," PEW Research Center, July 11, 2011. For European statistics, see Statista, "Smartphone User Penetration as Percentage of Total Population of Western Europe from 2011 to 2018," accessed January 10, 2017, https://www.statista.com/statistics/203722/smartphone-penetration-per-capita-in-western-europe-since-2000/. "It happened to": Andy Greenberg, "So Hey, You Should Stop Using Texts for Two-Factor Authentication," *WIRED*, June 26, 2016.

36. "Jon Oberheide, Duo's": In discussion with the author, September 30, 2016.

37. "US government agencies": The National Institute of Standards and Technology, which develops cryptographic standards and security guidelines for the non-national security side of the US government, recommends against text messages and in favor of secure smartphone apps for multifactor authentication; see Paul Grassi et al., *DRAFT NIST Special Publication 800-63B: Digital Identity Guidelines*, National Institute of Standards and Technology, January 9, 2017, section 5.1.3.2.

38. "Fortunately, these exist": The most popular is Yubikey, a hardware authentication device the size and shape of a door key.

39. "As one British": Shane Richmond, "Smartphones Hardly Used for Calls," *Telegraph*, June 29, 2012. "We increasingly": Robert Hof, "Apple Pay: A Clever Combination of Technologies Makes It Faster and More Secure to Buy Things with a Wave of Your Phone," *MIT Technology Review*, March/April 2015, accessed March 19, 2017, https://www.technologyreview.com/s/535001/apple-pay/.

40. "The bad news": Scott Wright, "The Symantec Smartphone Honey

Stick Project," 2012, accessed March 16, 2017, http://www.symantec.com/content/en/us/about/presskits/b-symantec-smartphone-honey-stick-project.en-us.pdf.

41. "Thieves stole 2": "Smartphone Thefts Drop as Kill Switch Usage Grows," *Consumer Reports*, June 11, 2015. The Federal Communications Commission reports lower numbers of thefts, but also explains that its survey may be underreporting; see Federal Communications Commission, *Report of Technological Advisory Committee (TAC) on Mobile Device Theft Protection (MDTP)*, Version 1.0, December 4, 2014, 6.

42. "Preventing the theft": Kevin Bankston, "The Numbers Don't Lie: Smartphone Encryption Will Help the Cops More than It Hurts Them," *Slate*, August 18, 2015, accessed March 16, 2017, http://www.slate.com/articles/technology/future_tense/2015/08/default_smartphone_encryption_will_stop_more_crimes_than_it_permits.html.

43. "For one thing": Matt Green, "The Limits of Android N Encryption," November 24, 2016, accessed February 24, 2016, https://blog.cryptographyengineering.com/2016/11/24/android-n-encryption/.

44. "In 2012, the": Internet Crime Complaint Center, "Smartphone Users Should Be Aware of Malware Targeting Mobile Devices and Safety Measures to Help Avoid Compromise," October 12, 2012, accessed February 3, 2017, http://www.ic3.gov/media/2012/121012.aspx; viewed at https://web.archive.org/web/20121014022840/http://www.ic3.gov/media/2012/121012.aspx. "In 2014, the": Mark Masnick, "FBI Quietly Removes Recommendation to Encrypt Your Phone . . . as FBI Director Warns How Encryption Will Lead to Tears," *Techdirt*, March 26, 2016, accessed February 3, 2017, https://community.webroot.com/t5/Security-Industry-News/FBI-Quietly-Removes-Recommendation-To-Encrypt-Your-Phone/td-p/194340.

45. Any complex digital device—a smartphone, a laptop, a thermostat, a car—needs software updates. The most important reason is patching vulnerabilities, but updates also serve to provide new functionality (which means you don't need a new phone every six months). And updates keep complex digital systems working as the other systems around them are updated and improved.

46. "When the FBI": The legal brief from the FBI discusses removing the security protections for the "SUBJECT DEVICE ONLY" (US District Court for the Central District of California, *In the Matter of the Search of an Apple iPhone Seized During the Execution of a Search Warrant on a Black Lexus IS300 California License Plate 35KGD203, ED No. 15–0451M, Government's Ex Parte Application for Order Compelling Apple Inc. to Assist Agents in Search*: Memorandum of Points and Authorities; Declaration of Christopher

Pluhar; Exhibit, 4). "Not about setting": James Comey, "We Could Not Look the Survivors in the Eye If We Did Not Follow This Lead," Lawfareblog.com, February 21, 2016. "But Apple's CEO": Tim Cook, "A Message to Our Customers," February 16, 2016.

47. "Weeks later, the": The Encryption Tightrope: Balancing Americans' Security and Privacy," Hearing before the House Committee on the Judiciary, 114th Congress (2016; James Comey, director, FBI), 47. "At the time": "The Encryption Tightrope: Balancing Americans' Security and Privacy," Hearing before the House Committee on the Judiciary, 114th Congress (2016; Cyrus Vance, Jr., New York County district attorney), 132. "Between October and": Adam Vaccaro, " 'You're Stuck with Me,' FBI Director James Comey Says," *Boston Globe,* March 8, 2017. The number 1,200 represents all devices received for forensic analysis through the FBI's Computer Analysis Response Team and the Regional Computer Forensics Labs (FBI communication with the author, March 23, 2017).

48. "To understand why": Apple, iOS Security: iOS 9.3 or later, May 2016, accessed March 8, 2017, https://www.apple.com/business/docs/iOS_ Security_Guide.pdf, 6.

49. It might appear that there is a discrepancy between the number cited above—1,200 phones in the fall of 2016—and the "tens of thousands" mentioned here. The FBI number was a partial survey of phones law enforcement had been unable to unlock; actual numbers were higher. The data was from 2016, when default-locked iPhones were only part of the market. As phones that are securely locked by default become even more common, the percentage of phones law enforcement can't open without technical help will increase. And that's only domestic. If the US government were to force Apple to develop software to unlock the phones, law enforcement globally would make the same demand.

50. "The more people": "The Encryption Tightrope: Balancing Americans' Security and Privacy," Hearing before the House Committee on the Judiciary, 114th Congress (2016; statement of Bruce Sewall, general counsel, Apple), 199–200.

51. I presented some of this argument during hearings on the Apple–FBI case: "The Encryption Tightrope" (statement by Susan Landau, professor, Worcester Polytechnic Institute), 122–23.

52. "Stolen private keys": Kim Zetter, *Countdown to Zero Day: Stuxnet and the Launch of the World's First Digital Weapon* (New York: Crown, 2014), 11–13 and 15–16.

53. "A 1999 study": Lance Hoffman, David Balenson, Karen Metivier-Carreiro, Anya Kim, and Matthew Mundy, "Growing Development of For-

eign Encryption Products in the Face of US Export Regulations," Cyberspace Policy Institute, George Washington University, June 10, 1999, accessed March 21, 2017, https://cryptome.org/cpi-survey.htm.

54. "The set was": The probability that the key would be reused in another communication was exceedingly small.

55. "The app uses": WhatsApp uses the Signal protocol, developed for secure phone calls. See https://whispersystems.org/, accessed January 14, 2017.

56. "It vastly improves": Cade Metz, "Forget Apple vs. the FBI: Whatsapp Just Switched On Encryption for a Billion People," *WIRED*, April 5, 2016.

57. "Nor has the": Telegram FAQ, accessed January 11, 2017, https://telegram.org/faq#q-how-is-telegram-different-from-whatsapp. "But 100 million": Telegram, "100,000,000 Monthly Active Users," accessed January 12, 2017, https://telegram.org/blog/100-million; and Joby Warrick, "The 'App of Choice' for Jihadists: ISIS Seizes an Internet Tool to Promote Terror," *Washington Post*, December 23, 2016.

58. "The website you're": Electronic Frontier Foundation, "Panopticlick," accessed January 12, 2017, https://panopticlick.eff.org/about.

59. "The onion router": The Tor Project, accessed January 12, 2017, https://www.torproject.org/.

60. "As the Tor": Roger Dingledine and Nick Mathewson, "Anonymity Loves Company: Usability and the Network Effect," The Fifth Workshop on Economics of Information Security (Pre-proceedings), June 26–28, 2006, accessed March 21, 2017, http://www.econinfosec.org/archive/weis2006/docs/41.pdf.

61. "A 2016 study": Bruce Schneier, Kathleen Seidel, Saranya Vijayakumar, "A Worldwide Survey of Encryption Products," Version 1.0, February 11, 2016, accessed March 21, 2017, https://www.schneier.com/academic/paperfiles/worldwide-survey-of-encryption-products.pdf.

62. "During the height": Dam and Lin, *Cryptography's Role in Securing the Information Society*, 6.

63. "As former NSA": In discussion with the author, November 4, 2016.

5

Investigations in the Age of Encryption

1. "They predicted that": Advanced Telephony Unit, Federal Bureau of Investigation, Telecommunications Overview, Slide on Encryption Equipment, 1992, 21, accessed January 17, 2016, https://www.cs.columbia.edu/~smb/Telecommunications_Overview_1992.pdf. "Encryption gained few":

The Administrative Office of the US Courts issues an annual report on wiretaps conducted in criminal investigations. Since 2001, these report any problems encountered with encryption. The reports show no difficulties with encryption even years later; *Wiretap Report 2011*, Table 7: Authorized Intercepts Granted Pursuant to 18 U.S.C. § 2519 as Reported in Wiretap Reports for Calendar Years 2001–2011. One should note, however, that if law enforcement is aware that the communication is encrypted, they may not seek a wiretap order. Encryption products were, however, rare during this period.

2. "According to the": Charlie Savage, "US Tries to Make It Easier to Wiretap the Internet," *New York Times*, September 27, 2010.

3. "FBI Director James": James Comey, "Going Dark: Are Technology, Privacy, and Public Safety on a Collision Course?" remarks delivered at Brookings Institution, October 16, 2014, accessed March 22, 2017, https://www.fbi.gov/news/speeches/going-dark-are-technology-privacy-and-public-safety-on-a-collision-course.

4. "Even though the": As is the case with many surveys, response depended on how the question was asked. See Phillip Elmer-Dewitt, "Apple vs. FBI: What the Polls Are Saying—Update," *Fortune*, February 23, 2016. "Favoring security over": Eric Lichtblau, "On Encryption Battle, Apple Has Advocates in Ex-National Security Officials," *New York Times*, April 22, 2016.

5. "Signals intelligence is": John Millis, staff director of the House Permanent Select Committee on Intelligence, made this comment during a speech at a Central Intelligence Retirees' Association Luncheon, October 5, 1999, *CIRA Newsletter*, Vol. 23, No. 4 (Winter 1998–99). "By the late": Neil King, Jr., "In Digital Age, US Spy Agency Fights to Keep from Going Deaf," *Wall Street Journal*, May 23, 2001.

6. "Microwave transmissions travel": In this situation, geography benefited the Soviet Union and hurt the United States. The former had an embassy in Washington and a summer vacation house on Long Island's north shore for its UN consulate staff. The combination was extremely well placed for eavesdropping on microwave transmissions along the US east coast. That's where the most important government and financial communications were most likely to pass. By contrast, the Soviet Union's vast land mass precluded a similar situation for US interception of Soviet microwave transmissions.

7. "RHYOLITE was in": Jeffrey Richelson, *A Century of Spies: Intelligence in the Twentieth Century* (Oxford: Oxford University Press, 1995), 328–29.

8. "Its deputy director": Interview, Rich Taylor by Gordon Lederman, December 10, 2003, 6, accessed December 10, 2016, https://cryptome.org

/nara/nsa/nsa-03-1210.pdf. "The NSA didn't": Sen. Bob Kerrey, Congressional Record Online via GPO Access, [DOCID:cr19jy99–96], S8790. "During the 1999": Robert Ackerman, "Security Agency Transitions from Backer to Participant," *SIGNAL*, October 1999, accessed December 10, 2016, https://www.afcea.org/content/?q=node/807.

9. "The agency hired" and "The agency's highly": Matthew Aid, "The NSA's New Code Breakers," *Foreign Policy*, October 15, 2013. "With TAO 'implants'": Craig Whitlock and Barton Gellman, "To Hunt bin Laden, Satellites Watched Abbattobad, Pakistan, and Navy SEALS," *Washington Post*, August 29, 2013.

10. "Report of TAO's": This was a step taken by the Russian Federal Guard Service, which is in charge of securing high-level state officials. Miriam Elder, "Russian Guard Service Reverts to Typewriters after NSA Leaks," *Guardian*, July 11, 2013.

11. "Or, as former": Ellen Nakashima, "Former National Security Officials Urge Government to Embrace Rise of Encryption," *Washington Post*, December 15, 2015. "And the 2017": WikiLeaks, Vault 7: CIA Hacking Tools Revealed, accessed March 8, 2017, https://wikileaks.org/ciav7p1/.

12. "As we have": The one exception was that CALEA was extended to cover Voice over IP communications for broadband access providers and interconnected VoIP services; see *American Council of Education v. Federal Communication Commission*, 371 U.S. App. D.C. 307; 451 F.3d 226. "In 2011, FBI" and "Communications at Twitter": "Going Dark: Lawful Electronic Surveillance in the Face of New Technologies," Hearing before the Subcommittee on Crime, Terrorism, and Homeland Security, House Committee on the Judiciary, 112th Congress (2011; statement of Valerie Caproni, FBI general counsel), 6–7.

13. "Mr. Issa: Did": "The Encryption Tightrope: Balancing Americans' Security and Privacy," Hearing before the House Committee on the Judiciary, 114th Congress (2016), 39–40.

14. "That is particularly": Rukmini Callimachi, "Not 'Lone Wolves' After All: How ISIS Guides Terror Plots from Afar," *New York Times*, February 4, 2017.

15. "State and local": Attorney General Eric Holder, Memorandum to the United States Attorney and Assistant Attorney General for the Criminal Division, Department Policy on Charging Mandatory Minimum Sentences and Recidivist Enhancements in Certain Drug Cases, August 12, 2013; and Lisa Sacco, *Drug Enforcement in the United States: History, Policy, and Trends*, Congressional Research Service, October 2, 2014, 21.

16. "One Texas investigator": Trey Oldham (investigator, Brazos County

Office of the Sheriff, Bryan, TX), in discussion with the author, January 14, 2017.

17. "But the Digital": Susan Landau, *Surveillance or Security? The Risks Posed by New Wiretapping Technologies* (Cambridge, MA: MIT Press, 2011), 99–104; and Peter Swire and Kenasa Ahmad, "Going Dark or a Golden Age for Surveillance?" November 28, 2011, accessed December 28, 2016, https://cdt.org/blog/%E2%80%98going-dark%E2%80%99-versus-a-%E2%80%98golden-age-for-surveillance%E2%80%99/. "In one sense": Patrick Brogan, US Telecom, "The Broadband and Mobile Transformation of US Communications," November 2012, accessed October 7, 2016, http://www.ustelecom.org/sites/default/files/documents/Voice%20Competition%20Slides%202012-11-15.pdf.

18. "A lot of": In discussion with the author, October 24, 2016.

19. "In France, police": Vanessa Gratzer and David Naccache, "Cryptography, Law Enforcement, and Mobile Communications," *IEEE Security and Privacy*, Vol. 4, No. 6 (November/December 2006), 68. "A determined Beirut": Ronen Bergman, "The Hezbollah Connection," *New York Times Magazine*, February 10, 2015.

20. "That the cell tower": *United States v. Antonio Evans*, 892 F. Supp. 2nd 949 (N.D. Ill 2012). "In 2014, an": *Lisa Marie Roberts, Petitioner v. Nancy Howton, Respondent,* in the United States District Court for the District of Oregon, 3:08-cv-01433-MA.

21. "Think back to": George Packer, "A Dirty Business: New York City's Top Prosecutor Takes on Wall Street Crime," *New Yorker*, June 27, 2011.

22. "In conjunction with": WikiLeaks, Vault 7: CIA Hacking Tools Revealed, Weeping Angel (Extending) Engineering Notes, accessed March 7, 2017, https://wikileaks.org/ciav7p1/cms/page_12353643.html. "In 2016, the": Spencer Ackerman and Sam Thielman, "US Intelligence Chief: We Might Use the Internet of Things to Spy on You," *Guardian*, February 9, 2016.

23. "I would find" and "The FBI had": Patrick Fitzgerald, "The Evolving Role of Technology in the Work of Leading Investigators and Prosecutors," Palantir, June 12, 2013, accessed December 12, 2016, https://www.youtube.com/watch?feature=player_embedded&v=Nd2fZZhxuzQ, .4:48–5:00.

24. "You figured out": Fitzgerald, "The Evolving Role of Technology in the Work of Leading Investigators and Prosecutors," 7:51–8:12.

25. "The US Organized": Fitzgerald, "The Evolving Role of Technology in the Work of Leading Investigators and Prosecutors," 11:39–12:44.

26. "A name might": Fitzgerald, "The Evolving Role of Technology in the Work of Leading Investigators and Prosecutors," 14:55–15:00.

27. "A lot of": In discussion with the author, December 6, 2016. "There's

legitimate wariness": Palantir briefly participated in a proposal to launch illegal cyberattacks against WikiLeaks supporters. It included disinformation against journalists. Palantir disavowed the plans once they became public, and fired the engineer involved—though they later rehired him. Quentin Hardy, "Unlocking Secrets, If Not Its Own Value," *New York Times,* May 31, 2014.

28. "A Los Angeles": David Gamero, "Palantir at the Los Angeles Police Department," June 12, 2013, accessed December 14, 2016, https://www.you tube.com/watch?v=aJ-u7yDwC6g, 1:28–2:05. "The tools help": Charlie Beck, "Palantir at the Los Angeles Police Department," 00:13–00:16. "Similarly, patterns of": Timothy Wargo, "Building a Human Trafficking Case from Lead to Arrest," June 12, 2013, accessed December 14, 2016, https://www .youtube.com/watch?v=gS1IMB-3dw.

29. "Using a cell": Kevin Bankston and Ashkan Soltani, "Tiny Constables and the Cost of Surveillance: Making Cents out of *United States v. Jones,"* *Yale Law Journal,* Vol. 123 (2012–14). "The broad availability": Techsafety. org, "Smartphone Encryption: Protecting Victim Privacy While Holding Victims Accountable," April 12, 2016, accessed February 2, 2017, https:// www.techsafety.org/blog/2016/4/12/smartphone-encryption-protecting -victim-privacy-while-holding-offenders-accountable, April 12, 2016.

30. "A former senior": In discussion with the author, September 15, 2016. "Other national security": Michael Hayden, in discussion with the author, November 4, 2016.

31. "In the United States": *Riley v. California,* 573 US 2473 (2014). "Britain's Scotland Yard": Dominic Casciani and Gaeten Portal, "Phone Encryption: Police 'Mug' Suspect to Get Data," *BBC News,* December 2, 2016.

32. "Within two days" and "Shortly afterwards, the": Scott Helman and Jenna Russell, *Long Way Home: Boston Under Attack, the City's Courageous Recovery, and the Epic Hunt for Justice* (New York: Dutton, 2014), 135. "The police published": Helman and Russell, *Long Way Home,* 148. "The bombers went": Helman and Russell, *Long Way Home,* 163.

33. "Anyone listening in": Tom Zeller, Jr., "On the Open Internet, a Web of Dark Alleys," *New York Times,* December 20, 2004.

34. "In 2007, Al" and "They developed additional": Eric Schmitt and Michael Schmidt, "Qaeda Plot Leak Has Undermined US Intelligence," *New York Times,* September 29, 2013.

35. "This was the": Don Van Natta, Jr., and Desmond Butler, "How Tiny Swiss Cellphone Chips Helped Track Global Terror Network," *New York Times,* March 4, 2004.

36. "Metadata is not": In discussion with the author, October 14, 2016.

37. "Ironically, the United States": Mark Mazzetti, Helen Cooper, and Peter Baker, "Behind the Hunt for bin Laden," *New York Times,* May 2, 2011.

38. "The Zeta cartel": Michael Weissenstein, "Mexico Cartels Build Own National Radio System," Associated Press, December 27, 2011. "Chertoff said": In discussion with the author, October 24, 2016.

39. "Many in the": "Police, Prosecutors Call for Fewer Arrests of Nonviolent Offenders," PBS *NewsHour,* October 21, 2015; and PEW Charitable Trust, "Federal Drug Sentencing Laws Bring High Cost, Low Return," August 27, 2015. "Thus encryption and": Interview with law enforcement source, September 20, 2016.

40. "Investigators instead used": "The Electronic Communications Privacy Act: Government Perspectives on Protecting Privacy in the Digital Age," Hearing before the Senate Committee on the Judiciary, 112th Congress (2012; statement of James Baker, FBI general counsel), 4.

41. "As we know": The NSA's efforts are directed against systems abroad, and the legal regime is somewhat different from the FBI's. The NSA strictly follows various legal and policy requirements including the Foreign Intelligence Surveillance Act (FISA), the FISA Amendments Act, the USA PATRIOT Act, decisions of the Foreign Intelligence Surveillance Court, and the United States Signals Intelligence Directive, USSID SP00018 (https://www.dni.gov/files/documents/1118/CLEANEDFinal%20USSID%20SP0018.pdf).

42. "Like all such": John Schwartz, "U.S. Refuses to Disclose PC Tracking," *New York Times,* August 25, 2001; and *United States of America v. Nicodemo S. Scarfo and Frank Paolercio,* United States District Court, District of New Jersey, Criminal 00–404, Affidavit of Randall S. Murch, October 4, 2011, accessed January 12, 2017, https://www.epic.org/crypto/scarfo/murch_aff.pdf.

43. "Although the key": *United States of America v. Nicodemo S. Scarfo and Frank Paolercio.* "In 2007 the": There was also an intrusion in 2003 that did not become public until 2016; see Matt Apuzzo, "FBI Used Hacking Software a Decade before iPhone Fight," *New York Times,* April 13, 2016. "The messages were": Kevin Poulsen, "FBI's Secret Spyware Tracks Down Teen Who Made Bomb Threats," *WIRED,* July 18, 2007.

44. "An FBI agent": Since that investigation, the FBI has tightened the rules under which an agent can impersonate a reporter; see Office of the Inspector General, Department of Justice, *A Review of the FBI's Impersonation of a Journalist in a Criminal Investigation,* September 2016, ii. "When the suspect": Office of the Inspector General, *A Review of the FBI's Imper-*

sonation of a Journalist in a Criminal Investigation, 1. "It simply provided": *In the Matter of the Search of Any Computer Accessing Electronic Message(s) Directed to Administrator of MySpace Account "Timberlinebombinfo" and Opening Message(s) Delivered to That Account by the Government*, United States District Court, Western District of Washington, Case 3:07-mj-05114-JPD, filed June 12, 2007, 4–5 and 13.

45. "In each of": Steven M. Bellovin et al., "Lawful Hacking: Using Existing Vulnerabilities for Wiretapping on the Internet," *Northwestern Journal of Technology and Intellectual Property*, Vol. 12, Issue 1 (2014). "Although the law": Law enforcement will also sometimes need what's known as a pen/trap order to collect the to/from, time, and date information.

46. "All law enforcement": The one exception would be if forward secrecy is used. Since each communication session has its own key, the device would have to leak the key for each one. "In fact, intelligence": They've been doing the same for landline phones—at least those on private branch exchanges (where the telephone switch belongs to a company, such as Macy's or Metropolitan Life Insurance, and not the phone company)—for close to thirty years.

47. "The FBI typically": FBI, Endpoint Surveillance Tools (released under the FOIA), https://www.eff.org/files/fbi_cipav-07-p50.pdf.

48. "Dutch police had": One way to achieve this is through a .onion address; see Tor Hidden Service Protocol, accessed March 5, 017, https://www.torproject.org/docs/hidden-services.html.en. "The Dutch investigators": *In the Matter of Search of Computers That Access the Website "Bulletin Board A" Located at http://jk pos24pl2r3ur]w.onion, Application for a Search Warrant*, United States District Court, District of Nebraska, https://www.documentcloud.org/documents/1261620-torpedo-affidavit.html (2012), 30; Kim Zetter, "Everything We Know about How the FBI Hacks People," *WIRED*, May 15, 2016; and Kevin Poulsen, "Visit the Wrong Website, and the FBI Could End Up in Your Computer," *WIRED*, August 15, 2014.

49. "But in Operation": *In the Matter of Search of Computers That Access the Website "Bulletin Board A" Located at http://jk pos24pl2r3ur]w.onion: Application for a Search Warrant*, United States District Court, District of Nebraska, 30; Zetter, "Everything We Know about How the FBI Hacks People"; and Poulsen, "Visit the Wrong Website, and the FBI Could End Up in Your Computer."

50. "In a court": *United States of America v. Ross Ulbricht, a/k/a "Dread Pirate Roberts," a/k/a "DPR," a/k/a "Silk Road," S1 14CR 68 (KBF), Declaration of Christopher Tarbell*, United States District Court, Southern District of New York (2014).

51. "Various technologists say": Krebs on Security, "Silk Road Lawyers

Poke Holes in FBI's Story," October 2, 2014; Errata Security, "Reading the Silk Road Configuration," October 3, 2014. "The FBI agent's": Marcy Wheeler, "The Temporal Problems with the Government's Story," October 11, 2014, accessed December 30, 2016, https://www.emptywheel.net/2014/10/11/a -remarkable-date-for-the-virgin-birth-of-the-silk-road-investigation/.

52. "They returned with": Joshua Bearman and Tomer Hanuka, "The Untold Story of Silk Road, Part II: The Fall," *WIRED* (June 2015). "By now the": *United States of America v. Ross Ulbricht, a/k/a "Dread Pirate Roberts," a/k/a "DPR," a/k/a "Silk Road," Sealed Complaint, Violations of 21 USC § 846, 18 USC 1030 & 1956,* United States District Court, Southern District of New York, September 27, 2013, 15.

53. "When the investigator": Bearman and Hanuka, "The Untold Story of Silk Road, Part II." "The user said": Nathaniel Popper, "The Tax Sleuth Who Took Down a Drug Lord," *New York Times,* December 25, 2015.

54. "His last known" and "While Ulbricht turned": Bearman and Hanuka, "The Untold Story of Silk Road, Part II."

55. "This, at least": Lillian Ablon and Andy Bogart, "Zero Days, Thousands of Nights: The Life and Times of Zero Day Vulnerabilities and Their Exploits," RAND Corporation, 2017.

56. "Indeed, the US": Michael Daniel, White House, "Heartbleed: Understanding When We Disclose Cyber Vulnerabilities," April 28, 2014, accessed March 8, 2017, https://obamawhitehouse.archives.gov/blog/2014/04/28/ heartbleed-understanding-when-we-disclose-cyber-vulnerabilities; WikiLeaks, Vault 7: CIA Hacking Tools Revealed, accessed March 8, 2017, https:// wikileaks.org/ciav7p1/.

57. "Lawful hacking is": Steven M. Bellovin et al., "Lawful Hacking: Using Existing Vulnerabilities for Wiretapping on the Internet," *Northwestern Journal of Technology and Intellectual Property,* Vol. 12, Issue 1 (2014).

58. "An Israeli company": Kim Zetter, "When the FBI Has a Phone It Can't Crack, It Calls These Israeli Hackers," *Intercept,* October 31, 2016.

59. "But Cellebrite also": Joseph Cox, "Hacker Dumps iOS Cracking Tools Allegedly Stolen from Cellebrite," *Motherboard,* https://motherboard .vice.com/en_us/article/hacker-dumps-ios-cracking-tools-allegedly-stolen -from-cellebrite, February 2, 2017, accessed December 20, 2016.

60. "Cellebrite builds devices": Zetter, "When the FBI Has a Phone It Can't Crack"; Cellebrite, "Unlock Digital Intelligence: Accelerate Investigations Anywhere," accessed December 20, 2016, http://www.cellebrite.com/Media /Default/Files/Forensics/Solution-Briefs/Mobile-Forensics-Solution-Brief .pdf. "The company's technology": Zetter, "When the FBI Has a Phone It Can't Crack."

61. "'Smartphone extraction'": Cellebrite, "Cellebrite Smart Phone Extraction," accessed January 18, 2017, https://www.cellebritelearningcenter.com/mod/page/view.php?id=11286.

62. "The tools made" and "After Zdziarksi's analysis": Jonathan Zdziarski, "An Example of Forensic Science at Its Worst: US v Brig. Gen. Jeffrey Sinclair," August 24, 2014, accessed December 25, 2016, https://www.zdziarski.com/blog/?p=3717.

63. "In a financial": James Verini, "The Great Cyberheist," *New York Times Magazine,* November 10, 2010.

64. "They focus instead": Law enforcement official in background discussion with the author, December 28, 2016. "in 2015 alone": The conviction data is from Federal Bureau of Investigation, US Department of Justice, FY 2017 Authorization and Budget Request to Congress, 4–30; the estimate of losses due to Internet fraud is from Federal Bureau of Investigation, US Department of Justice, *2015 Internet Crime Report,* 12.

65. "Within weeks, however": Sam Gibbs and agencies, "FBI bought $1m iPhone 5C Hack, but Doesn't Know How It Works," *Guardian,* April 29, 2016. "His total cost": Sergei Sorogobatov, "The Bumpy Road Towards iPhone 5c NAND Mirroring," accessed September 15, 2016, https://arxiv.org/abs/1609.04327. "Cellebrite also claimed": Zetter, "When the FBI Has a Phone It Can't Crack."

66. "Agents wanted": Jonathan Zdziarski, in discussion with the author, December 9, 2016.

67. "The 2017 budget": Federal Bureau of Investigation, US Department of Justice, FY 2017 Authorization and Budget Request to Congress, 5–7.

68. "In 2015 the": District Attorney, New York County, *Report of the Manhattan District Attorney's Office on Smartphone Encryption and Public Safety,* November 2015, 7.

69. "There are all": National White Collar Crime Center, *Cybercrime Investigations,* accessed February 7, 2017, http://www.nw3c.org/classroom-training/cybercrime-course-list.

70. "Not to be" and "NDCAC's hotline is": Betsy Glick (FBI) email to the author, February 6, 2017. "A lot of": Interview with the author, February 10, 2017.

71. "Despite calls for": "Going Dark: Lawful Electronic Surveillance in the Face of New Technologies," Hearing before the Subcommittee on Crime, Terrorism, and Homeland Security, House Committee on the Judiciary, 112th Congress (2011; statement by Susan Landau, Radcliffe Institute), 35 and 43. Others were pressing for this as well, but the effort took a long time

to bear fruit; see Mark Greenblatt and Robert Cribb, "FBI Opens New Chapter in 'Going Dark,'" *Herald,* November 14, 2015.

72. "This law-enforcement": This is based on 18 USC § 1029 and 18 USC § 1030. "The devices come": Carlo Allegri, "Hunting for Evidence, Secret Service Unlocks Phone Data with Force or Finesse," *Passcode,* February 2, 2017.

73. "With a quarter": Jeff Roberts and Robert Hackett, "Exclusive: Inside America's Newest Digital Crime Lab," *Forbes,* November 16, 2016.

74. "That the director": "The Encryption Tightrope: Balancing Americans' Security and Privacy," Hearing before the House Committee on the Judiciary, 114th Congress (2016; statement of Susan Landau, professor, Worcester Polytechnic Institute), 15.

75. "Law enforcement should": This is based on my testimony at "The Encryption Tightrope," 106.

6
There's No Turning Back

1. "In 1993, the": Adam Bryant, "COMPANY REPORTS: Times Co. Reports Income of $10.9 Million," *New York Times,* April 14, 1993; Sydney Ember, "New York Times Co. Reports Loss as Digital Subscriptions Grow," *New York Times,* May 3, 2016; Sydney Ember, "New York Times Co. Reports an Advertising Drop, Though Digital Results Grew," *New York Times,* November 2, 2016.

2. "In the decade": Aaron Smith, Lee Rainie, Kyley McGeeney, Scott Keeter, and Maeve Duggan, "US Smartphone Use in 2015," Pew Research Center, April 1, 2015, 33.

3. "These war games": US Department of Defense, "Cyber Guard Exercise Tests People, Partnerships," July 17, 2014, accessed February 10, 2017, https://www.defense.gov/News/Article/Article/602897; US Department of Defense, "Cyber Guard 15 Fact Sheet," accessed February 10, 2017, https://www.defense.gov/Portals/1/features/2015/0415_cyber-strategy/Cyber_Guard_15_Fact_Sheet_010715_f.pdf; Karen Parrish, "Cyber Guard 2016 Seeks to Manage Complexity in an Invisible Domain," June 18, 2016, accessed February 10, 2017, https://www.defense.gov/News/Article/Article/803018/cyber-guard-2016-seeks-to-manage-complexity-in-invisible-domain.

4. "But actions by": Kertu Ruus, "Cyber War I: Estonia Attacked from Russia," *European Affairs,* Vol. 9, Issue 1–2 (Winter/Spring 2008), http://www.europeaninstitute.org/index.php/component/content/article?id=67:cyber-war-i-estonia-attacked-from-russia; Ronald Diebert, Rafal Rohozinski, and

Masahi Crete-Nishihata, "Cyclones in Cyberspace: Information-shaping and Denial in the Russia-Georgia War," *Security Dialogue*, Vol. 43, No. 1 (2012), 12. "Similarly, the 2015": Peter Behr and Blake Sobczak, "The Hack: Utilities Look Back to the Future for Hands-on Cyberdefense," *EENews*, July 21, 2016, accessed March 23, 2017, http://www.eenews.net/special_reports /the_hack/stories/1060040590.

5. "But the Soviet": It should be noted that the press was also not free under the tsars. However, the level of control and propaganda vastly increased in the Soviet Union. "In creating the": Perhaps the best demonstration of this can be seen in the 1976 film *Man of Marble* by the Polish director Andrej Wajda. "Central to this": A particularly good account of this may be found in Scott Shane, *Dismantling Utopia: How Information Ended the Soviet Union* (Chicago: Ivan. R Dee, 1994).

6. "US intelligence agencies": Office of the Director of National Intelligence, *Background to "Assessing Russian Activities and Intentions": The Analytic Process and Cyber Incident Attribution*, January 6, 2017.

7. "In 2015, the": *Hearing on the Nomination of Joseph Dunford for Commandant of the Marine Corps before the Senate Committee on Armed Forces*, 114th Congress (2015), accessed January 27, 2015, https://www.c-span.org /video/?c4548676/general-dunford-threat-russia-poses-nothing-short -alarming, 0:07–0:09. "Six months later": *Hearing on Foreign Cyber Threats to the United States before the Senate Armed Forces Committee*, 114th Congress (2016; prepared statement, James Clapper, director of national intelligence), 1. "As Clapper testified": *Hearing on Foreign Cyber Threats to the United States before the Senate Armed Forces Committee*, 5.

8. "A group supposedly": Angelique Chrsafis and Samuel Gibbs, "French Media Groups to Hold Emergency Meeting after Isis Cyber-attack," *Guardian*, April 9, 2015, and Gordon Corera, "How France's TV5 Was Almost Destroyed by 'Russian Hackers,'" *BBC News*, October 10, 2016.

9. "One quick-thinking": Corera, "How France's TV5 Was Almost Destroyed by 'Russian Hackers.'"

10. "They ran false": Andrew Higgins, "It's France's Turn to Worry about Election Meddling by Russia," *New York Times*, April 17, 2017; and Alex Hern, "Macron Hackers Linked to Russian-Affiliated Group behind US Attack," *Guardian*, May 8, 2017.

11. "But to Russia": Rod Thorton, "The Changing Nature of Modern Warfare: Responding to Russian Information Warfare," *RUSI Journal*, Vol. 160, No. 4 (August/September 2015).

12. "Once again, the": Dmitry Gorenburg, "Countering Color Revolutions: Russia's New Security Strategy and Its Implications for U.S. Policy,"

Russian Military Reform, September 15, 2014, accessed March 22, 2107, https://russiamil.wordpress.com/2014/09/15/countering-color-revolutions-russias-new-security-strategy-and-its-implications-for-u-s-policy/; and Thorton, "The Changing Nature of Modern Warfare." "The government worried": Dmitry Gorenburg, "Countering Color Revolutions"; and Thorton, "The Changing Nature of Modern Warfare."

13. "Where the Western": Graphic from Gerasimov article in *Voyenno-Promyshlennyy Kurier,* Vol. 26 (February 2013), translated by Charles Bartles in Thorton, "The Changing Nature of Modern Warfare."

14. "In the early": Gorenburg, "Countering Color Revolutions." "In 2013 Russia's": Nathan Hodge, James Marson, Paul Sonne, "Behind Russia's Cyber Strategy: A 2013 Article by Gen. Valery Gerasimov Emphasizes Importance of Cyberwarfare," *Wall Street Journal,* December 30, 2016. "Russia would blur": Charles Bartles, "Getting Gerasimov Right," *Military Review,* 2016, accessed March 22, 2017, http://usacac.army.mil/CAC2/MilitaryReview /Archives/English/MilitaryReview_20160228_art009.pdf; and Gen. Robert Neller, speech at Center for Strategic and International Studies, August 9, 2016, accessed March 22, 2017, https://www.c-span.org/video/?413764-1 /general-robert-neller-discusses-maritime-security, 54:15–54:17. "There'd be no": Neller, speech at Center for Strategic and International Studies, 54:23–54:36.

15. "The government began": Andrew Kramer, "How Russia Recruited Elite Hackers for Its Cyberwar," *New York Times,* December 29, 2016.

16. ""Russia is not": Carlo Maria Rossoto et al., *A Sector Assessment: Broadband in Russia,* International Bank for Reconstruction and Development/World Bank, January 2015. "And US military": This is required under the Laws of Armed Conflict, but the US military observes this prohibition even when there is no declared war.

17. According to US": James Clapper, *Foreign Cyber Threats to the United States: Hearing before the Senate Armed Forces Committee,* 5 (2017); "Or as the": Natalie Nougayrède, "Watch Out, Europe: Germany Is Top of Russian Hackers' List," *Guardian,* January 13, 2017.

18. "What if, instead": James Clapper, Statement for the Record, Worldwide Cyber Threats, House Permanent Select Committee on Intelligence, September 10, 2015, 5. "What if the": MIT Center for International Studies and MIT Internet Policy Research Initiative, *Keeping America Safe: Toward More Secure Networks for Critical Sectors: Report on a Series of MIT Workshops, 2015–2016,* 35. "Factory antics in": *"Modern Times*: Factory Scene Late Afternoon," 1936, accessed February 3, 2017, https://www.youtube.com /watch?v=HPSK4zZtzLI.

19. "Then in 2015": White House, "Remarks by President Obama and President Xi of the People's Republic of China in Joint Press Conference," September 25, 2015. "China signed a": Adam Segal, "The US-China Espionage Deal One Year Later," Council on Foreign Relations, September 28, 2016, accessed March 22, 2017, http://blogs.cfr.org/cyber/2016/09/28/the -u-s-china-cyber-espionage-deal-one-year-later/.

20. "But to virtually": FireEye iSight Intelligence, "RedLine Drawn: China Recalculates Its Use of Cyberespionage," June 2016. "The importance of": *United States of America v. Wang Dong, a/k/a "Jack Wang," a/k/a "Ugly Gorilla," Sun Kailiang, a/k/a "Sun Kai Liang," a/k/a "Jack Sun," Wen Xinyu, a/k/a "Wen Xin Yu," a/k/a "WinXYHappy," a/k/a "Win_XY," a/k/a "Lao Wen," Huang Zhenyu, a/k/a "Huang Zhen Yu," a/k/a "hzy_lhx," and Gu Chunhu, a/k/a "Gu Chun Hui," a/k/a "KandyGoo,"* Criminal No. 14–118, 18 USC § 1030 (a) (2) (C), 1030 (a) (5) (A) 1030 (b), 18 USC § 1028A, 18 USC 1831 (a) (2), (a) (4), and 18 USC § 1832 (a) (2), United States District Court, Western District of Pennsylvania, filed May 1, 2014; Ellen Nakashima, "US Developing Sanctions against China over Cyberthreats," *Washington Post*, August 30, 2015.

21. "Improvement is definitely": Ralph Langner and Perry Pederson, *Bound to Fail: Why Cyber Security Risk Cannot Simply Be "Managed" Away*, Computer Security Series, Brookings Institution, February 2013, 11. "Currently the systems": Langner and Pederson, *Bound to Fail*, 7–8. "Russia is believed": Jordan Robertson and Michael Riley, "Mysterious '08 Turkey Pipeline Blast Opened New Cyberwar," *Bloomberg Technology*, December 10, 2014.

22. "In any government": Abraham Lincoln, Gettysburg Address, November 19, 1863. "sine qua non": Jean Cohen, "Trust, Voluntary Association, and Workable Democracy," in Mark Warren, ed., *Democracy and Trust* (Cambridge: Cambridge University Press, 1999), 216. "That includes emails": Sam Biddle, "Top Secret Snowden Document Reveals What the NSA Knew about Previous Russian Hacking," *Intercept*, December 29, 2016, accessed March 23, 2017.

23. "Political scientists observe": Robert Putnam, *Making Democracy Work* (Princeton: Princeton University Press, 1993). "US intelligence agencies": Office of the Director of National Intelligence, *Assessing Russian Activities and Intents in Recent US Elections*, Intelligence Community Assessment, January 6, 2017.

24. "Indeed, the *Wall*": Mara Gay, "Messaging App Has Bipartisan Support amid Hacking Concerns; Aides to Trump, Obama and de Blasio use Signal, a Smartphone App that Encrypts Messages," *Wall Street Journal*, January 24, 2017.

25. "Regardless of how": Committee on Responding to Section 5(d) of Presidential Decision Directive 28: The Feasibility of Software to Provide Alternatives to Bulk Signals Intelligence Collection, *Bulk Collection of Signals Intelligence: Technical Options* (Washington: National Academies Press, 2014), 15–25.

26. "In testifying to": *The Encryption Tightrope: Balancing Americans' Security and Privacy; Hearing before the House Committee on the Judiciary,* 114th Congress (2016; statement by James Comey, FBI director), 56. "But the best": New America Foundation, *Terrorism in America after 9/11, Part IV: What Is the Threat to the United States Today?* accessed January 26, 2017, https://www.newamerica.org/in-depth/terrorism-in-america/what-threat -united-states-today/.

27. "Our greatest threat": Dan Magan, "Intelligence Boss Clapper: Russia Poses 'Existential Threat' to the United States," accessed March 23, 2017, http://www.cnbc.com/2017/01/05/sen-mccain-everyone-should-be -alarmed-by-russia-hacks.html.

28. "Signal saw a": Note that this does not mean, of course, an equivalent increase in use. Jeff John Roberts, "This Messaging App Saw a Surge after Trump's Election," *Fortune,* December 2, 2016.

29. "Cloud computing services": Claire Cain Miller, "Revelations of NSA Spying Cost US Tech Companies," *New York Times,* March 21, 2014.

30. "Former Department of": In discussion with the author, October 24, 2016.

31. "Political espionage by": See, for example, Carl Bernstein and Bob Woodward, *All the President's Men* (New York: Simon and Schuster, 1974).

32. "On a number": *Final Report of the Select Committee to Study Governmental Operations with Respect to Intelligence Activities: Supplementary Detailed Staff Reports on Intelligence Activities and the Rights of Americans,* S. Rep. No. 94–755, Book II (1976), 15–16. "Yet voices of": S. Rept. 94–755, Book II (1976), 291.

33. "Each individual": Leonard Levy, *Seasoned Judgments: The American Constitution, Rights, and History* (Piscataway, NJ: Transaction, 1997), 307.

34. "If that article": Eight states had prohibited general warrants within their own constitutions by the time the US Constitution was ratified; William Cuddihy, "Historical Origins of the Fourth Amendment," Leonard W. Levy and Kenneth L. Karst, eds., *Encyclopedia of the American Constitution* (New York: MacMillan Reference, 2000), 1,099.

35. "not to prevent": My thinking on the Fourth Amendment as a security amendment has been influenced by Jed Rubenfeld, "The End of Privacy," *Stanford Law Review,* Vol. 61 (2008–2009), 104.

Acknowledgments

It is nearly seven years since Sun Microsystems went out of existence, but I felt its powerful influence as I was writing this book. I first began thinking about cryptography policy while working with Whit Diffie, and that fruitful collaboration continues to impact how I think about encryption issues. Greg Papadopoulos guided me in thinking about atoms as bits and bits as atoms; Dave Edstrom, about wiring the factory floor; Hal Stern, about bits and healthcare. James Gosling once told me Sun was the best graduate school he'd ever attended—and it was for me as well.

I've many people to thank for their help. I am indebted to Kevin Bankston, Steve Bellovin, Niels Provos, Ari Schwartz, John Treichler, and Karen Utgoff, who asked me many hard and pointed questions; their search for truth improved an earlier draft (all remaining errors are mine, of course). Many people gave generously of their time, even when they didn't always know why I was asking certain questions. This includes Dirk Balfanz, Doug Bellin, David Bitkower, Matt Blaze, Courtney Bowman, Clint Brooks, Erika Calabrese, Michael Chertoff, Marty Edwards, Kathleen Fisher, Al Gidari, John Grant, Eric

Grosse, Mike Hayden, Josh Hearen, Ralph Langner, Herb Lin, Richard Littlehale, Paul Martinez, Mark Melson, Erik Neuenschwander, Trey Oldham, Tim Roxey, Rick Salgado, Bill Sanders, Bruce Sewall, Peggy Speas, Jim Stewart, Rebecca Taylor, Paul Tiao, Mary Wirth, Ben Wittes, Tony Wolfe—and a number of people, in and out of government, who prefer to remain anonymous. This book was written while I was at Worcester Polytechnic Institute, and I am grateful for their gracious support. I'd also like to thank the Radcliffe Institute for Advanced Study; my year there taught me to think in new ways.

With *Listening In*, I was aiming for a new audience. If I met the challenge, it is due to the incomparable Audra Wolfe, who worked magic on my ideas and prose. I was extremely lucky to have her by my side.

My husband, Neil Immerman, said, "Sure, write a book in six months. I'll do everything else." Well, yes, he could have raked more of last autumn's leaves. But he cooked every meal, read innumerable drafts, retrieved reference materials more times than I can count, and encouraged me in every way possible. His multiple generosities sped me on my way.

Index